PATIENT CATALYST

Leading Church Revitalization

Jack L. Daniel

Overseed PRESS

Patient Catalyst
Published by Overseed Press
A Division of William & James Publishing
581 Washington Street, #3
South Easton, MA 02375

ISBN 9781940151038

Cover Design: Sparrow Design Studios

To my wife Kathryn,

my partner and heir with me in "the gracious gift of life."

FOREWORD

If you drive north on I-89 from Hanover, NH, in about 20 miles you will pass Sharon, VT. From the interstate you can see a quintessential white church set against the beautiful green mountains. This is a picture replicated across almost every town in New England. The church on the green is a familiar New England sight.

Unfortunately, the beautiful outside picture of these churches does not match the inside realities. Many of these New England churches are no longer flourishing. They have shifted theologically from the historical gospel and drifted from missional call of Jesus. A large number are on the brink of closing

A recent study of New England concluded that 41% of churchgoing Christians in New England are non-practicing and display such generally low levels of spiritual vitality that they and their churches are equally important audiences for evangelism and discipleship as the many non-Christians in New England. Revitalization is a key missional strategy for helping to reach New England for Christ again. Certainly, the great need for revitalization extends beyond New England to the rest of the United States.

As Jack will lay out in the upcoming chapters, the key factor in revitalizing these churches is a pastor who is a patient catalyst— someone who will shepherd the current congregants and be a catalyst for a new gospel centered ministry in the community. Jack, a seasoned revitalization pastor himself, provides us with great pastoral advice about leading the process of revitalizing a church in this timely book. He lays out the patterns and timeframes that typically accompany revitalization. The reader will do well to pay attention to my friend Jack's advice.

I have known Jack for almost ten years, first as a board member of Overseed. He was the senior pastor of Free Christian Church in Andover, MA, where he had revitalized a dying congregational church. Under his leadership, the church grew back to health, and over his 35-year tenure the church grew to be a multi-site congregation of over a thousand.

Then, second, when Jack retired from pastoring, he became Overseed's first Field Director. Jack's wisdom, experience, and friendship have been key to the success of Overseed. As we have co-labored together, Jack has helped me guide Overseed as we build a network of coaches focused on coaching revitalization pastors in New England.

In the pages that follow, you will get a front row seat into what it is like to pastor a church back to health as a patient catalyst. My prayer is that Jack's experience and wisdom will both challenge and encourage you to either take up the mantle or continue the course of revitalization. The church needs more patient catalyst pastors who love God's church and can lead it back to health by God's grace!

Dr. Jim Harrell
President, Overseed

PREFACE

Many years ago, I was a newly minted pastor in a church that was not only in serious decline but had actually talked about closing its doors. They took a chance on a young pastor and called me to my first and only pastorate. Soon I joined a small group of pastors, most of whom were also young and serving declining churches. We would meet monthly to study God's word, to pray, and mostly to complain about how hard our work was. One of our members was a little older and a little further along in the renewal of his church. One day, after hearing enough of our complaining, he told a story that transformed my understanding of revitalization ministry.

He said, "Imagine that you are part of a church planting denomination in the South that wants to send you to New England to plant a church. They assure you they will do several things to make it easier for you to start a church. One, they will guarantee a salary and benefits. Two, they will provide you with rent-free housing. Three, they will find you a church building in a strategic location in the community. Four, they will supply you with a small congregation who are committed to being part of the church. Five, included in the congregation will be a remnant of committed believers. Six, they will give the church a name, a positive identity in the community, an organizational structure, and some leaders to help you run the church. This hypothetical church planting denomination asks only that you lead the rest of the church members to Christ, disciple them and then lead the church in its mission to the community." Then he dropped the bombshell: "That is precisely your situation; that is what God has given you;

and all you can do is complain. Why don't you recognize that you are a missionary to your church and get on with lovingly and patiently leading your congregation back to Christ."

That anecdote put the whole task of revitalization into a new and proper perspective for me. It is essentially a missionary calling, and like all missionaries, we have to work within the culture, accept where our people are, lead them patiently to where God is calling them, and be realistic about how long it is going to take.

That story also showed me I needed a coach, someone who was further along on the journey of church renewal than I was. I needed a guide who could help me see the big picture of what God was doing and to understand the somewhat predictable pattern that church revitalization follows. In addition to the Holy Spirit who is everything, such a coach is essential to the task of church revitalization—someone who has traveled the road of renewal before and can serve as a mentor, speaking clarity into the otherwise cloudy complexities of the task. Coaching the next generation of revitalization pastors in New England is the main work of Overseed, the ministry I work with.

Acknowledgments. Most of the people who have influenced this book won't ever know how, or how much, they have helped me. I am most grateful to my congregation at the Free Christian Church in Andover, MA, who for 35 years loved and prayed for me and helped form Christ in me. It was a labor of love to pastor them. More than any expert or mentor, they shaped my understanding of church revitalization. I also owe a debt of gratitude to Jim Harrell, the founder and president of Overseed, who gently insisted that I write this book. Finally, I want to thank my wife Kathryn, who as a professional editor helped put this book in its final form and of course is my companion on life's journey.

JLD, July 2018

CONTENTS

SEASON FOUR: THE FRUITFUL YEARS
A TIME TO FLOURISH

SEASON FIVE: TRANSITION
A TIME FOR DEPARTURE OR REINVENTION

1

"Restoring What Has Been Lost"

Some people restore antique furniture, others antique cars, still others antique houses. God is in the business of restoring congregations. In this book I will use the words *revitalize, replant, renew,* and *restore* interchangeably. I believe all of them convey roughly the same idea. I know that the word *replant* has come to have the connotation of a new church plant taking over a declining church building or location. However, I do not think that is the best or most likely way that God will renew his church. We need that kind of renewal, and we need new church plants. But in my view, the greatest opportunity for revival in America lies in the revitalization of the many thousands of existing churches in decline.

I like all of the ways God is rebuilding His church, and all of the terms for that process, but my favorite word for the work is *restore.* The word *restore* is rich in biblical and church history. Time after time, the Prophets of Israel called God's people back to

1

obedience and national restoration. In the Book of Revelation, Jesus calls the seven churches of Asia Minor back to their first love and spiritual restoration. Since the beginning, churches have gone through the stages of birth, growth, plateau, decline, and rebirth. Christian history is the story of the church being restored after it has fallen into decline. It is the story of the church "reformed and reforming." The word *restoration* is especially fitting with regard to church revitalization because it suggests that God is bringing something back that worked in the past and will work again in the future. It implies that church revitalization is not about blowing up the past to create something totally new. Instead, it is about holding onto the treasures of the past while seeing God do something new with them.

The dictionary definition of *restore* is "to bring something back to its previous state, or original condition." The key idea is to go back to the beginning, rediscover the original design, and make that work again today. Church restoration means rediscovering the original design of the church as we find it in the pages of the New Testament. A revitalization pastor has to go back and recapture God's purpose for the church because, chances are, the reason a church is in decline is because it has drifted from that purpose. The pastor can also go back and find the reason for the existence of his or her particular church. Why was this church planted in the first place? Was it to minister to a certain segment of the population? Was it to disciple people won to Christ in a revival? Was it planted as a mission-sending church? Recapturing that founding vision is often vital in calling a congregation back to the covenant God made with them.

When people restore a piece of furniture, a car, or a house, they strive not only to recapture the original design but also to make the item more functional for the modern world. The piece of furniture will have a new durable finish, the car may have a state-of-the-art electronic ignition, the house will have modern wiring and plumbing. So it is with the restoration of a church. The original purpose does not change, but the methodology does. Restoration will bring the church culture and practice up-to-date so it can function in today's world.

A book on church revitalization is nothing new, but church revitalization is more needed now in our country than ever before. Aubrey Malphurs, professor of leadership and pastoral ministry at Dallas Theological Seminary, declares in his book *Planting Growing Churches for the 21st Century* that 80 to 85 percent of all U.S. churches are either plateaued or declining (2004, p. 12). Thom Rainer challenges that number based on a recent survey of 1,000 churches. He says the number is closer to 65 percent. While that figure is a little more encouraging, it still means that two-thirds of all the churches in America are in need of revitalization. (Thom Rainer Newsletter, July 5, 2017). It is estimated that 200 churches are closing every week, more than 10,000 a year. Meanwhile, the number of new churches planted each year is about 4,000. That's a net loss of 6,000 churches annually. In New England, more than half of the 7,400 Protestant churches are in serious decline and in need of revitalization. The mainline denominations—such as the American Baptist Church, the United Methodist Church, and the United Church of Christ, to mention a few—are all continuing a 50-year decline in membership. According to a 2015 internal study done by the United Church of Christ, there will be an 80 percent loss of church membership by the year 2045. This trend is probably true for the other mainline denominations. This means that thousands of historic, strategically located church buildings will become restaurants, retail space, condos, or simply torn down. To paraphrase Martin Luther, "Why should the devil get all the good property?" At Overseed, the nonprofit ministry organization I work with, we are praying that God calls thousands of biblically orthodox, "patient catalyst" pastors to fill the pulpits of declining churches. We believe that church revitalization, along with church planting, represents a huge opportunity to bring revival to America.

This opportunity is being recognized by church planting organizations that realize the value of renewing existing congregations versus the challenge of starting new one. Both church plants and church revitalizations have their place, but a revitalization usually comes with a building and often a good location. In addition, the church belongs in the community and does not have to justify why the community needs another church. Church revitalizations often have a glorious history of godly, faithful Christian pioneers who covenanted with God to start a church. We believe that God keeps his covenants, and when a church body rededicates itself to that covenant, God blesses that church. Recently, Gordon-Conwell Theological Seminary, after decades of teaching church planting courses, began offering a course in church revitalization. The school is actively encouraging students to consider a call to a declining church, with the belief that God is faithful to His covenants.

ASSUMPTIONS

I make several assumptions about my readers:

- First, that you have a persevering desire to see a specific church or all declining churches revitalized. Otherwise, you probably would not be reading this book.
- Second, that you are committed to Jesus Christ as your Lord and Savior.
- Third, that you believe that the proclamation of the Gospel and making disciples constitute the primary mission of the church.
- Fourth, that you believe that God answers prayer and that you are praying specifically and generally for God to renew His church.
- Finally, that you have been called in some capacity to be part of the revitalization of the Church.

These assumptions form the foundation for the ideas I propose in the following chapters. I make these assumptions because without faith in Jesus Christ and His word, and without persistent prayer and persevering effort, church revitalization is unlikely to happen. There is no human program that can bring it about.

Church revitalization is not easy because churches are complex organizations. Ministry is increasingly difficult, and in my opinion, revitalization ministry has never been more challenging. The reasons are evident:

- The breakdown of marriage and the family means many more hurting people are drawn to the church seeking hope and healing, and pastors struggle to care for them.
- The increasing mistrust of institutions and authority figures in our culture creates a bias against church organizations and leadership.
- The unrealistic expectations projected onto leaders in every arena, from politics to the pastorate, puts tremendous pressure on leaders.
- A huge generational shift is taking place as the Builder generation (the "greatest" generation, victors of World War II) is nearly gone, but many churches still operate on an outmoded ministry model based on this generation's culture. And the Boomer generation that has pastored most churches for the last 40 years is also aging away and leaving thousands of empty pulpits.
- The post-Christian, post-denominational, post-attractional church culture of America signals that the days of easy church growth are probably behind us.
- The financial burden of supporting a full-time pastor (and family) and the soaring costs of maintaining church buildings are beyond the reach of most churches in America.

- Many churches have or will have bi-vocational pastors, which creates further problems with revitalizing.
- Finally, the millions of immigrants entering our country often bring their own Christian church cultures with them.

All these factors and others are putting enormous pressure on the declining church in America and on those who long to see it renewed.

This book is an attempt to offer some hope that the same Lord who spoke life into the drifting churches of 1st-century Asia Minor can speak life into the declining church in America in the 21st century.

This is the ministry of Overseed. Founded in 2008 by Dr. Jim Harrell. While the focus of Overseed is to help revitalize churches in the six-state New England region, we believe the need for church renewal exists everywhere in America. I believe that the dynamics and process of church revitalization also apply to the thousands of churches across the country longing to be renewed.

THE SEASONS OF REVITALIZATION

Because the God revealed in both Scripture and Creation is a God of order and process, it should be no surprise that we can detect an order and process to the seemingly chaotic work of church revitalization. I firmly believe that the renewal of a declining church follows a somewhat predictable model. While each church revitalization is unique, there are patterns and a process. Because of this, we can look at how God has worked in other places, through other people, in other times, and gain hope and guidance for the work of renewal.

I compare the revitalization process to a marriage and use five seasons of a marriage to help orient us to the seasons in a church revitalization. In Ephesians 5 the Apostle Paul compares the relationship of marriage to the relationship of Christ and the Church. We could wish that Paul had said more, but he simply leaves off by calling this comparison a "mystery." New Testament scholar F. F. Bruce calls the comparison a "parable." The marriage relationship is a parable about the relationship of Jesus Christ and His people. Evidently, marriage with all of its beauty and imperfection helps us understand the perfect relationship between Jesus and the human soul even as it is lived out imperfectly in this world.

My comparison of the process of church restoration to a marriage is not profound. In fact, it's pretty simple. Just as there are seasons in a marriage, so too there are seasons in the life of a church. Beginning with the Engagement and ending with a Renewal of Vows, I describe each season of church revitalization hoping that the analogy will make it easier for revitalization pastors to discern where they are in the church renewal process. The time frames I have attached to the various seasons of church revitalization are only rough approximations. They may in fact vary greatly, but these parameters can serve as a general guide. It will take more time or less to lead a church back to health, depending on many factors that we will discuss.

Season One: The Engagement

The "engagement" is the period *before* you say yes to a church, the time when you are discerning if you are called to revitalization in general and to this church in particular. In both a potential marriage relationship and a potential ministry relationship, it is during the engagement that we try to decide if the proposed match is a good fit. In a romantic relationship, this process takes place largely at an intuitive and even subconscious level as two people decipher feelings of attraction and compatibility in personalities, histories, values, and interests. Rarely does a dating couple have to resort to a list of pros and cons in making their decision. In a church, it is different. There needs to be a time for clarifying expectations, calling, theology, and compatibility. Typically, a pulpit committee compiles a list of questions to ask a pastoral candidate; likewise, the candidate should be equipped with a list of questions for the church. Part one of the book, or Season One, deals with this so-called engagement period. Thorough, thoughtful discernment in this period can lay the groundwork for healthy renewal later on.

Season Two: The Honeymoon
In a marriage, a honeymoon immediately follows the wedding. It's a time for intimacy and mutual enjoyment as partners discover one another. In a church setting, "honeymoon" is popular parlance for the early period in a pastoral ministry—say the first two years—when much grace is extended to a pastor and the pastor acts with great patience toward the congregation. During the honeymoon, the congregation and the pastor have an irretrievable window in which to build mutual trust. Unfortunately, this grace period is often misunderstood, and trust is *not* established.

Season Three: The Early Years
In a marriage, this season corresponds to the early years when a couple gets down to the business of making their life together work. Add in the pressure of careers and child rearing, and it is easily the most stressful season in life. In a church, it is in this time frame that revitalization pastors must begin their most important task: leading a church through change. It is in this phase of renewal that conflict typically ensues. The conflict is almost inevitable, but the length and intensity of this period depends largely on the pastor's leadership skills, his or her spiritual and emotional health, and the spiritual and emotional health of the congregation.

Season Four: The Fruitful Years
In a marriage, this season begins the long period when a couple has found a way to create a satisfying and productive life together. In a church revitalization, it is a time when new life is beginning to be catalyzed, revitalization is taking hold in a congregation, and the church is experiencing some numerical and spiritual growth.

This is what a pastor longs for and what the Holy Spirit of Christ produces as He renews His Bride. In my view, if clear signs of revitalization have not emerged after 10 years, renewal (under this pastorate, at least) is unlikely to happen. Although renewal is an ongoing process because the church of Jesus Christ is always a reformed and reforming church, a church does reach a point where it can be said to be revitalized. It most likely occurs within this season of a pastorate.

Season Five: Transition—Departure or Reinvention

In a marriage, when most of a couple's life work is done, children are raised, careers are winding down, there is a time of reinvention when a couple must find new reasons for being married. Sometimes a couple symbolizes this fresh start with a renewal of their wedding vows. Sadly, it is often at this point that husband and wife fail to navigate these uncertain waters and instead go their separate ways. In a church, once the hard heavy lifting of renewal is completed, a pastor and congregation must reinvent their relationship. In a church, it is also often at this point, just when the greatest potential for further vitality and effectiveness exists, that congregations and their pastors also part ways. A deliberate reinvention of roles might give a pastor new vision and the staying power for a long-term ministry.

This comparison of a church to a marriage is apt given the fact that a church is a family system. I am indebted to the late Rabbi Edwin Friedman for his work in understanding churches as family systems. That the church is a family system, in fact the only eternal family system, is seen in the language of the New Testament. The Apostle Paul calls the church the "household of God" (Ephesians 2:19) and "God's family in heaven and earth" (Ephesians 3:15). The Apostle Peter refers to the church as a "spiritual house" (I Peter 1:5). John calls the church the "bride of Christ" (Revelation 19:7; 21:2). Paul speaks of the relationship between a husband and wife as illustrating the profound mystery of the relationship between Christ and His people. Paul also compares relationships within in the church to the relationships in the human family (I Timothy 5:1-2).

Friedman suggests that is important for a pastor to understand that beginning a new pastorate is like marrying into a large, blended family. It is as though the pastor is the new husband in a marriage in which the bride has been married many times before and brings all the history of those previous marriages with her into. This is only an analogy since Jesus Christ, not the pastor, is the church's husband, and pastors must not foster dependence on themselves but on Christ. However, it is helpful to think in terms of a large blended family in which the congregation has had deep relationships with many other pastors in the past. The nature of those relationships will help a new pastor comprehend his or her relationship with the church.

. . . . .

When we understand that God has made a church a family system and that, like every family system, it is looking for leadership, we can begin to decode church complexity and have hope that pastoral leadership is what is needed.

It is my prayer that this book will make a small contribution to the understanding of church revitalization and be an encouragement to the thousands of faithful pastors called to this ministry of "restoring what has been lost."

2

Asking the Right Questions

In his 1985 book *Generation to Generation*, Rabbi Edwin Friedman compares the period when a pastor is discerning a specific call to that pre-wedding time in a couple's relationship: the engagement (Friedman, p. 253). In a romantic relationship, the couple has already discovered at an intuitive level the potential for marriage. But in a prospective pastor-church relationship, the pastor must undertake a prayerful, rational approach to the call and have eyes-wide-open conversations with the church.

First and foremost, a pastor needs to assess his or her calling and gifting for the specific task of a replanting ministry. Recognize that to revitalize a church is a sacrificial calling, not just another ministry opportunity (Harrell, *Church Replanter*, p. 163). It involves a call and a long-haul commitment to a particular declining or dying church with particular issues.

11

I use the term "patient catalyst" to describe what a replant pastor is. Replant pastors are patient chaplains among the existing congregation, but they must also eventually catalyze a new congregation within the existing one. If a pastor is mostly a patient chaplain, the church will continue on its trajectory of decline. If a pastor is mostly a dynamic catalyst, the church may split, and either he or she will leave, or a segment of the congregation will. A replant pastor must be both a patient shepherd and a determined change agent, wisely gauging when to push forward and when to back off.

Second, remember that as a pastoral candidate being interviewed, you are interviewing the church as well. You need to formulate in your mind all the questions you will address with the search committee as you try to come to an understanding of their history, expectations, hopes, and dreams. Many of these questions should be asked in an indirect way in conversations with the committee or church leaders, not all at once but over time, meeting with them on several occasions. If applicable, denominational officials can be helpful, too.

Often pastors mistakenly focus all their questions on the future, as in "Does the church recognize the need to change?" or "Does the church want to reach out to younger families?" All congregations in need of revitalization will answer yes to such questions, and they will be sincere. But they have not begun to count the cost of undertaking these kinds of actions. Only when a pastor tries to lead will the real cost of change be realized, and often then will it be vigorously resisted.

The better approach is to begin by asking questions about the church's past. This will allow you to get a sense of the course the church has been on and the values it has embraced over time. I would suggest some of the following questions:

1. How long was the previous pastor there, and why did he or she leave? You may even want to ask this about the two

previous pastors, especially if their tenures were short. Remember, as Friedman says, you are marrying into a large blended family and the previous pastors have probably left a complicated and sometimes messy "residue" (p. 253).

2. Is the previous pastor still in the church or living in the community? If so, this could be a deal breaker for you. I believe a former pastor should separate from the church for at least a year. If a previous pastor has no plan to do that, you may want to look for another call. It is nearly impossible for a previous pastor who stays on to remove himself completely from a pastoral presence in the life and workings of his former church. In my view, it is rarely helpful to have the former pastor in the congregation.

3. Ask how the previous pastor(s) were regarded. As with a previous marriage, the church may have grieved the end of the relationship, or it may have welcomed it. If pastors have tended to leave after short stays, the congregation may have some "separation" issues and may assume your tenure will also be short.

4. Ask about the lines of authority in the church. Who are the power brokers, or "tribal chiefs," to use Lyle Schaller's term. Who has to give their permission to get things done? Ask this in a positive way, as in "Who are the real church leaders, as opposed to the committee heads?" Ask the committee chairs to describe their business meetings in one word.

5. What are the financial resources of the church? Can they afford a full-time pastor, or is it a part-time position? Remember, there are no part-time ministries, only part-time salaries. Can they afford benefits such as medical insurance, a retirement package, an expense account? Do they provide housing, or can they help a pastor with a down payment on a house? These are not necessarily deal

breakers. Many a pastor has had to start with part-time ministry compensation and little else. Realistically ask yourself if you can live on the salary package the church is offering. Do not assume that the package will increase over time. You do not want to put your family in jeopardy or begin to resent your congregation when the financial struggle comes. Go into the interview knowing what your family needs.

6.   Thom Rainer suggests handing out index cards to the search committee and asking each person to write his or her top three expectations for a pastor. Then prayerfully consider if these match your expectations of your role. Do the respective expectations align? If not, then it may not be a good match. If they do match, then have a frank discussion and record everything in writing; the day may come when you will need to recall what was agreed on for yourself and for the church.

7.   Ask about the church's founding vision. Often historical churches were founded for very noble and godly reasons— perhaps to evangelize a segment of the community, or to serve the poor, or to equip and send missionaries. That history may be leveraged to lead the church forward, saying, "We HAVE done this before!"

8.   Ask about church splits or other traumatic events, such as moral failures on the part of pastors or leaders. What has been done to heal these? Ask the oldest members of the church to recall the happiest and saddest times in the church.

9.   What is the theological history of the church? What is its current theological makeup? If there is a wide divergence theologically between you and the congregation, it may not be a good fit. Realize that congregations are rarely as theologically liberal or conservative as their pastor. And make sure you are speaking the same language. Do you

and the committee have the same understanding of terms such as *liberal, evangelical, fundamentalist,* and the like? I have been called both a liberal and a fundamentalist, although I am neither!

10. What has been the church's relationship with the outside community and with other local churches? How do church members and leaders view the community and, in particular, the other local churches?

In addition to inquiring about the church's past, find out what you can about where the church is today. The following questions will help you explore different aspects of the church's current status. This will be the starting point for any revitalization efforts you undertake, so don't go in blind.

1. What would the committee say are the church's greatest strengths and weaknesses?
2. How much do they recognize the need for change? In declined churches, the congregation focuses mostly on their own needs, not the needs of others, so do not be surprised if they are looking for a chaplain more than a catalyst.
3. Look at the church's worship service, the liturgy, and the music, and make sure you are comfortable enough with them to live with the status quo for a while. If you accept the call, you should resist the temptation to make any major changes to the service until you have won the trust of the congregation. Changing the worship service too soon is the "third rail" of church revitalization, and many a good pastor has "electrocuted" himself on this issue.
4. What is the "size culture" of the church? Is it a family size church with average Sunday attendance (ASA) from 3 to 75? Is it a pastoral size church with ASA from 76 to 140, or is it a program size church with ASA from 200 upward?

Do they think of themselves as a small church? Were they once a large church, and do they still think that way? It is often easier to revitalize a Pastoral size or Program size church than a Family size church. I will say more about how size dynamics affects the renewal of a church in the next chapter.

5. What is the age demographic of the church? It is very difficult for people in their 70s and 80s to change. Younger pastors should imagine how their parents or grandparents would react to the kinds of changes they are envisioning.

6. What is the cultural, socioeconomic, and/or ethnic makeup of the congregation? Is it a good fit for you? Recognize that in a blue-collar congregation you may have people who are used to taking orders and may willingly follow your lead, but who struggle to provide leadership themselves. In a largely white-collar congregation, on the other hand, you may have more educated entrepreneurial people who know how to lead and get things done, but who may resist pastoral leadership.

7. What is the surrounding community like? Does the church reflect it? Has the community changed around the church, leaving it as a cultural "backwater"? Over time, a healthy church can identify with the surrounding culture and, by evangelizing that population, can reflect the makeup of the local community.

8. Will you be able to live in the same community as the church? It is important for a pastor in a replant situation to identify with the local community that he or she is trying to reach for Christ.

9. What is the facility like? Has it been well maintained, or is it in need of major repair? Is the building in a visible and accessible location? Is there adequate parking either on site or in close proximity? Take these facility questions seriously, because while not insurmountable, they can have

a significant impact on whether this church can be revitalized.

10. What are the church's expectations for your spouse and children? Have you had a family meeting with them about your call and this church? Do the church's expectations align with your family's expectations?

11. Has the church shown evidence of strong dependence on the Holy Spirit through prayer as it considers or embarks on change? How have the congregation and leadership been praying about these matters (for example, through small gatherings or special prayer events)? Has there been some concerted, congregation-wide prayer about the issues that need to be addressed for the future? How well-attended have these events been?

Spend time, effort, and prayer in consultation with your spouse and trusted advisors in this Engagement Season. Do not be desperate. Take your time, trust God's call, and make a good choice. The words of the prophet Haggai remind us that if we are called to revitalize, we are to focus our efforts on rebuilding the LORD's church, not on fulfilling our personal, self-aggrandizing dreams of building a large church and a celebrated ministry: "Then the word of the Lord came through the prophet Haggai: . . . 'You expected much, but see, it turned about to be little. What you brought home, I blew away. Why?' declares the Lord Almighty. 'Because of my house, which remains a ruin, while each of you is busy with your own house'" (Haggai 1:3, 9).

3

Understanding the Starting Point

The most critical information to discern in the Engagement Season is your starting point, or more precisely, the church's starting point. Clearly, not all revitalization churches are the same, and not all start from the same turnaround point. Understanding the "starting point" for your church's renewal process is essential. The Apostle Paul reminds us that, in the church in Corinth, he "planted, Apollos watered, but God gave the increase." Some churches are already further along a path of renewal, thanks perhaps to the efforts of a previous pastor.

Here are some issues to consider in identifying the starting point of a replant church.

- Would your presence represent a change in the theological direction of the church, or did a predecessor begin that process? It is very difficult to be the *first* conservative or evangelical pastor in a church that has a long history of theologically liberal pastors. However, as stated earlier, most congregations are neither as liberal nor as conservative as their pastor.

- Does the church have enough members and leaders to continue carrying out the basic functions of the church?
- Is there some diversity in the age makeup of the church? If all of the leadership is elderly, leading the church through change will require more patience.
- Is the church financially stable? Or will it likely run out of money within the first few years of your pastorate?
- Is there a sense of urgency about needing to change the direction of the church in order to survive? Or is there complacency and resignation to an inevitable demise?
- What is the "size culture" of the church? Probably the most critical factor in determining the starting point for renewal is the church's understanding as it relates to size. Kevin Martin's *The Myth of the 200 Barrier* analyzes this phenomenon with great insight. In terms of size culture, churches can be conveniently divided into three basic categories: family size, pastoral size, and program size. (Program size churches can be further classified into small program, medium program, and large program types.) Let's examine each size in detail.

THE FAMILY SIZE CHURCH

Family size churches have an average Sunday attendance (ASA) ranging from 3 to 75, with a median of 35 (Martin, p. 30). They are made up of a few families, function like a single cell, typically have a part-time pastor, and make up the vast majority of churches in America. Some 46 percent of American churchgoers attend family size churches (Barna, 2016). Their identity is wrapped up in their history, relationships, and traditions, not in their pastor. The members are bonded to the church and to Christ through their family connections.

Think of a family size church like a pet cat. Both are independent, sometimes aloof, and able to fend for themselves for long periods of time. One of the chief characteristics of the family size church is its ability to function without a pastor. In fact, supply preachers and interim pastors can enable a family size church to maintain its existence indefinitely. These churches can carry out the functions of a church themselves, only needing a pastor to preach and to perform baptisms, weddings, and funerals. As a result of this independence, family size churches are in my opinion the most difficult to revitalize because they resist the effort of a pastor to lead. Family size seems to be the default position of a church. Over time, without pastoral leadership, most churches will naturally decline to a family size.

But wait. Weren't all the New Testament churches family size? This is a question that New Testament scholars have long asked. Scripture gives us a few clues; for example, we are told that the churches in Jerusalem and Antioch were very large. Beyond that, all we know is that house churches were the norm. Roman era archaeology reveals that houses were mostly single room structures with one, two, or three stories. Only in the church in Jerusalem is there a reference to multiple house churches. Is it safe to assume that the size of houses would limit most New Testament churches to family size? Most likely. I believe a case can also be made about the smallness of the New Testament church from the social dynamics we see in some of Paul's letters. For instance, the conflict in the Philippian church between two women required Paul to address it from Rome. Further, the incestuous behavior of one man in Corinth needed to be addressed by Paul in two letters. In large churches, the negative influence of one or two individuals is muted or diluted. If the churches in Philippi and Corinth were large, then the issues could probably have been handled at the local level. I am encouraged to think that, even in the age of the Apostles, churches were small, but of course we will probably never know for sure.

On the Positive Side

Healthy family size churches have wonderful strengths, such as a deep sense of community, a genuine care for one another, an "all hands on deck" participation by the members, and an ability to enfold a limited number of outsiders and to offer compassion to broken people who come into the fellowship.

These churches value such qualities as everyone knowing everyone else, people having priority over programs, maintaining the church property, being financially solvent, being faithful in worship attendance, financial support of the church, and the ability to support a part-time pastor. They value the status quo and maintaining the traditions of the past. Even without a pastor, they can lead themselves, up to a point and at least for a while. A healthy family size church may be the most pure expression of Christian community.

On the Negative Side

Unhealthy family size churches assume that their pastor will not stay long and are reluctant to let him or her lead. They suffer from low self-esteem and are often threatened by large churches around them. But they don't need to be. Large churches have large back doors, and many people struggle to find their place of belonging in such large settings. A healthy small church can be a very attractive place for these displaced churchgoers. My church was located within easy driving distance of the largest megachurch in New England, and we both lost members to it and gained members from it. Overall, though, we gained more than we lost.

In an effort to embrace all the members, family size churches will often tolerate bad behavior on the part of a few. They will sacrifice quality in worship and programming in favor of participation. They are suspicious of newcomers unless they are related to church members or bring value to the church through leadership skills or financial resources. They are focused on the needs of the congregation, not on the needs of the unchurched in the wider community. They often have a history of conflict, church splits, and numerical decline. The congregation is often elderly and out of sync with the demography of the surrounding community. They feel nostalgic toward the "good old days" and believe that recapturing the past will lead to renewal. They often have odd or eccentric worship traditions that give meaning to members but are exclusionary to newcomers. In a family size church worship service, members may feel free to stand and make impromptu announcements, or offer prayer concerns, or in more charismatic settings, to speak in tongues or voice a so-called prophecy or word of knowledge. To the members, this all seems normal, but to visitors or newcomers whom the pastor is trying to win to Christ, it seems weird and off-putting. This behavior fairly guarantees that the church will stay small and unrenewed, which may be why the Apostle Paul cautioned against this haphazard practice in I Corinthians 14.

Challenges to Revitalizing a Family Size Church
The following factors make it very difficult to revitalize a family size church.

1. *Control:* Typically, a few families or individuals control family size churches; they resist yielding leadership to a pastor; and they make it difficult for new leaders to emerge. If a pastor is prepared to be very patient and win the support of the leaders, then revitalization is not only possible, but also likely.

2. *Part-time pastoral leadership:* It is simply very hard to have a full-time job outside the church and pastor part-time. A revitalization church requires more time and more energy than other churches, but a part-time pastor has less time and less energy available. A pastor might be wise to seek a full-time position in another church or raise up lay leaders to help with the renewal.

3. *Trust:* Family size churches have trust issues due to a history of short pastoral tenures. Because these churches are continually saying goodbye, they do not bond deeply with a pastor. However, if a pastor is called to stay for the long haul, then trust can be built.

4. *Independence:* A family size church has learned how to function without a pastor and can maintain the status quo almost indefinitely. This independence can be a good thing as members are willing and able to lead vital functions in the church.

5. *Age:* Family churches are usually comprised of older congregations, making them more set in their ways and making it more difficult for the church to attract younger families. A wise revitalization pastor can encourage an older congregation to shift into the role of spiritual grandparents and turn leadership over to the next generation.

6. *Internal focus:* Family churches are highly focused on meeting the needs of the existing members. Since this takes so much effort, there is little energy left to care about those outside the fellowship. However, if a replant pastor can inspire the congregation to obey Christ's Great Commandment and Great Commission, the depth of community they experience can attract outsiders.

7. *Consensus required:* Major decisions are difficult to make in a family size church because everyone must be consulted even for minor issues. A pastor must learn to win over the "tribal chiefs" and then allow them to bring the congregation on board.

8. *Lack of quality:* Because the church functions like a family, with everyone accepted as they are, unskilled or poorly trained people are put in leadership roles. The lack of quality in the worship and programs of a family size church are off-putting to visitors and outsiders. The most

important and easiest thing a replant pastor can do to improve the quality of worship is to accurately preach the word of God with skill and passion. It is the one church activity he has complete control over. He can also patiently teach the theology of spiritual gifts and pray for God to raise up the gifts the church needs to get healthy.

The problems associated with revitalizing a family size church are daunting. But the vast majority of replant pastors are called to smaller churches. Take heart! A pastor who is willing to patiently earn trust *can*, over time, lead a family size church back to a place of true Christian community that will attract outsiders.

"Who despises the day of small things?" (Zechariah 4:10). As I talk to pastors of family size churches, I am aware that many are ambitious to see their churches grow larger. There is nothing wrong with ambition; after all, growth represents human beings, men, women and children, made in the image of God with an eternal destiny, coming to know Christ. However, the goal ought not to be growth, but health. Rick Warren's slogan is helpful: "Health is the goal, balance is the key (among the five purposes of the church), and growth is the result." Signs of health would be characteristics such as a Christ-centered mission, zeal for souls, joyful worship, biblical preaching, a strong sense of belonging, a grace-filled and forgiving congregation, dependence on Christ, a high degree of trust, and members serving according to their gifts. My wife and I worship in a healthy family size church, and it is a place of rich blessing for us.

THE PASTORAL SIZE CHURCH

Pastoral size churches have an average Sunday attendance that ranges from 76 to 140, with a median of 110, and 60 to 80 family units. They make up the second largest number of churches in

America. They have a pastor-centered identity and are organized to provide for the pastor's support.

Think of a pastoral church like a pet dog. Both are eager to spend time with their leader; both are good at following commands; but both are very dependent on their master (pastor) for their care and feeding. The chief characteristic of a pastoral church is that it is too big to lead itself. It must depend on pastoral leadership. In a pastoral church, high value is placed on everyone knowing the pastor and having access to him, as well as everyone knowing one another. Also, the pastor is typically tasked with providing overall leadership and direction. Pastoral churches have a traditional understanding of the role of the pastor and expect their pastor to show support by being present at all church functions and to be active in parish visitation and pastoral care. Pastoral churches value long pastoral tenure; thus, they grieve the loss of the previous pastor and often compare the current pastor to him or her. Moreover, pastoral churches become anxious when they are without a pastor. This can lead them to make hasty decisions when seeking a new pastor. In my view, pastoral churches are easier to revitalize than family churches because considerable authority to lead has already been given to the pastor.

On the Positive Side
Pastoral size churches are able to support a full-time pastor. Also, they are willing to follow a pastor's lead. They are big enough to allow visitors and newcomers to quickly become integrated. Further, they can provide ministry to children and youth, two very important factors for families seeking a healthy church home.

On the Negative Side
A pastoral church will rarely grow beyond 150 ASA unless it changes considerably. This is because 150 is the approximate number of people whom the average pastor can effectively relate to and lead. This number seems to be hard-wired into the

psychosocial makeup of human beings. It is observable in other leadership-dependent social systems such as tribes, military units, and corporations. In a pastoral size church, the pastor is the gatekeeper, and people are drawn to the church through him because of his personality, often feeling that he is their close friend. They are also drawn because of his ministry skills, especially preaching. The individual members are connected to the church because of and through the pastor. He is the glue that holds everyone together. Consequently, as the membership exceeds the pastor's capacity to relate meaningfully to everyone, some members will start to disengage, feeling that the pastor does not have time for them anymore. A frequent complaint is that "the pastor pays too much attention to newcomers." Further, in a pastoral size church, the pastor inadvertently becomes a bureaucratic bottleneck for the development of the ministry. Because everyone defers to the pastor for approval and blessing, everything takes longer to happen.

Challenges to Revitalizing a Pastoral Size Church

What happens when a pastoral church reaches its growth ceiling of around 150 and the pastor starts to hear complaints about not spending enough time with the people? The pastor's natural tendency is to absorb the blame and double-down, giving more time to visiting, counseling, and other pastoral care duties. This pretty much guarantees that the church will plateau. A better approach would be to teach the congregation that it is God who is "giving the increase," that this is His blessing and an opportunity for *everyone* to discover, develop, and deploy their gifts. The pastor must shift from being a shepherd to the people and become a shepherd to the shepherds—those volunteer and paid leaders who are providing care to groups within the congregation. The pastor must become the leader of leaders. So instead of trying to be all things to all people, the pastoral focus is now on some people more than others, developing leaders who will in turn help shepherd the flock. In this way, the pastor increases his or her span of care. If a pastor is persevering in teaching the biblical role of pastor as the "equipper of the saints for the work of ministry" (Ephesians 4:12), a pastoral size church can be revitalized and can transition into the next size, the program size church.

If you are considering revitalizing a pastoral church, ask yourself if you are successfully able to minister to people in small groups, avoiding conflicts. Are you able to bring about biblical reconciliation among individuals?

THE PROGRAM SIZE CHURCH

Program size churches have an average Sunday attendance of 200 to 400. The chief characteristic of this size church is that the members are primarily bonded to the church and Christ through ministries or programs aimed at meeting human needs. Unlike in family size or pastoral size church, the glue that holds the congregation together is not family relationships or the senior pastor but rather the ministries and those who lead and participate in them. In a program size church, it is not uncommon to see people seated on a Sunday morning with members of their small group. There is no expectation that you will know everyone, or that you will have immediate access to the pastor. Instead, the expectation is that you will be bonded with others who are in the same ministry with you. Think of the program size church like a team of draught horses, yoked together and working in tandem to accomplish a lot more work than the cat or dog, but needing direction and a high degree of coordination.

A major characteristic of a program church is an expectation of excellence. As the church grows from a small program church to a medium program (ASA of 400–600) and from medium to large program (ASA 600–900), the quality of all the functions of the church must increase.

Also, the leadership structure of the church must become more streamlined. In fact, a program church is led largely by professional staff, not elders, because the church is now too complex and fast moving for volunteer elders to keep up with day-to-day events and decisions. The elders' role shifts from leadership to guidance, policymaking, conflict resolution, church discipline, and protection of the staff. In a program church, the pastor spends time coaching and supporting the church staff of paid and volunteer leaders and striving to build Christian community among them. If cohesion, unity, trust, and affection are present at this staff level, it will permeate the whole church. Conversely, there are few things so destructive to a program church than major conflict and division among the staff.

In my opinion, a program size church is the easiest for a pastor to lead because he or she is given considerable authority. And these churches are the easiest to grow as institutional momentum increases. The transition from a small to a medium to a large program church is smoother than going from a family to a pastoral church, even though the growth involves vastly larger numbers. This kind of numerical growth is enabled by factors such as favorable demographics in the surrounding region, the gifting of the senior pastor to undergo major reinventions of his role, and of course a special and often mysterious empowering of the Spirit.

. . . . .

Engagement is a time for honesty, transparency, and realism about today, as well as hope for tomorrow. It is the season for heart-to-heart talks with the church about what God is calling each party to be and do. Ask the right questions, even the hard ones. Discover all you can about the church, so you will have a realistic appreciation of the starting point. Above all, be honest with the congregation about your intention to preach the whole counsel of God and to apply the word of God to lives individually and to the church collectively. The freedom to preach the Gospel of Jesus Christ from the whole Scripture is the one precondition a pastor must establish in a replant church.

Take your time to discern your call to a ministry of revitalization. As Overseed founder Dr. Jim Harrell says, "Typically the work is too hard, the resulting conflict is too draining, and the duration of the project is too long to be sustained by earthly motivations. It requires the replanter to be crystal clear about the call" (p. 32).

4

Laying a Foundation of Trust

We use the term "honeymoon" in many job settings, not just the pastorate, to describe a beginning period when relationships are open and hopeful and when judgment is suspended. In a marriage, the honeymoon follows the wedding as a time of discovery, a time for newlyweds to celebrate and establish trust in a relaxed vacation setting before beginning the hard work of life together as husband and wife. In a pastoral ministry, the honeymoon follows the acceptance of a call and is also a time of discovery, when a pastor and congregation are getting to know each other and building mutual trust and affection. Each party, open and hopeful, wants the relationship to work. It is so important for a pastor to understand the meaning of the honeymoon and to use it for appropriate purposes.

THE REASON FOR THE (HONEYMOON) SEASON

The honeymoon season consists of roughly the first couple of years of a pastorate. Usually, a congregation is willing to extend this grace period to a pastor. After all, they have selected this person to be their shepherd following a long, prayerful, and often difficult or painful process. They want this relationship to succeed. So the honeymoon constitutes a period of high hopes for both the church and their new shepherd.

The congregation is waiting and watching to see who this person they have called is. Clearly, the whole search process—as thorough as it might have been—did not reveal everything about their candidate. During the honeymoon, then, judgment is suspended and favor is extended to the pastor. A wise pastor will appreciate this honeymoon phase. It offers a wonderful window of opportunity for establishing and strengthening trust . . . in the context of the status quo. This trust will be much needed further along in the ministry to lead the congregation through the changes necessary for renewal, when the status quo will doubtless be upset.

A huge danger for pastors is to misunderstand the purpose and opportunity that a honeymoon represents for their ministry. As pastors, we are tempted to misinterpret the favorable climate of the honeymoon as acceptance of the agenda we are bringing. When the pastor's ideas are greeted with smiles and nods at a board meeting, the pastor may mistakenly assume the board is in agreement. But just because a call was extended does not mean there is a mandate for change.

After more than 40 years of ministry in replant situations, I am convinced that the most common mistake that replant pastors make—and it is often a disastrous one—is to try to introduce significant change during the honeymoon season. The honeymoon is for creating a foundation of trust and mutual affection. If a pastor builds this foundation, the process of leading change later on will be that much easier.

Conventional wisdom was that the honeymoon is a time to "rip off the bandage" quickly. In other words, if major change is needed, then do it soon and get it out of the way. This has often been the advice given to new pastors. I am guilty of trying this strategy myself. It may have worked in the past, but in this current culture in declining churches, there are too many hurting people and too much suspicion of organized religion as well as the motives of pastors. Honeymoons should not be rushed. Rule number one is "Go Slow," and rule number two is "Don't Forget Rule Number One."

To make major changes at the beginning of a pastor-church relationship is to take unfair advantage of the season of favor the congregation has extended. The better response is simply to love, or learn to love, the people God has called you to shepherd. It is expressed in the old saying, "People don't care what you know until they know that you care." There will be plenty of time to lead the change needed to reverse the downward trend of a declining church. The honeymoon is not that time. That said, the honeymoon is not an idle period, though it may seem so. Building trust and learning to love your people happen as you are actively engaged, not passively biding your time.

My experience and observation have taught me some helpful strategies for beginning well in a pastorate. Here is my list of "dos" for the pastor-church honeymoon. In the next chapter, I'll suggest what NOT to do in this season.

RECOMMENDATIONS FOR BUILDING TRUST

Be patient. This is the "patient" part of The Patient Catalyst. The catalyzing time will come soon enough; now is the time for patience. Two words in the New Testament are translated as our word patience. The first is often translated as "perseverance." It has to do with our relationship to our circumstances, where we need to "hang in there" in the challenges of ministry. The second word is often translated as "longsuffering." It has more to do with our relationship to people. Literally it means "long anger"; in other words, this kind of patience involves having a long fuse in those difficult, potentially explosive, encounters with certain people. Both aspects of patience are necessary if you are a pastor called to revitalize a church. You need to persevere in the difficult circumstances you face, and you need a long fuse when dealing with difficult and sometimes angry people you are called to serve.

It is during the honeymoon that your pastoring is like that of a chaplain caring for the people where they are. At this stage, the congregation is not looking for a catalyst but for someone who will care for them. Remember, they were leading the church in the interim before you arrived, and possibly for a long time before that. They may not have led it well, as a family system really cannot lead itself. But for now, they want to know that you love them and will be Christ's person as they go through the changes of life. For now, your job, like the one Jesus assigned to Peter, is to "feed my sheep." And you will feed them primarily as you give them the word of God on Sundays and as you meet them in their homes and workplaces and in the functions of the church.

Maintain regular office hours. The members of your congregation need to feel they have access to you, even if it is only on one day a week. Knowing when you are in your office makes it easier for them to reach you. Preferably, your office hours should be at the church. Having your office in your home creates a barrier for people. When people do not know the facts, they can assume the worst. If they cannot see you working, they may assume you are not working.

Visit all your members. In my first pastorate I had an inactive, elderly congregation of about 350, while Sunday attendance averaged 70. With my part-time secretary setting up appointments, I visited all 350 in a little over a year. Since they were largely retired, I would make my visits during weekday afternoons. I recall with fondness the leisurely pace of my ministry then, having afternoon coffee or tea and hearing the stories of these dear folks who had grown up during World War I and the Great Depression, who had lost sons in World War II, who had worked in the textile mills of the Merrimack Valley of Massachusetts. Sometimes I would bring my wife or my small children along. I would read Scripture, pray with them, and ask them to pray for me and the church. I believe that I was able to build much needed trust in those early years that would gain me the support of these saints in later years.

Think of your flock as family. In the early days of my ministry, some of my parishioners were two and even three times as old as I was. I had to think of them like I would think of my parents or grandparents. This made me more patient with them, knowing how hard it would be for my parents to adjust to the changes needed to bring the church back to life. The Apostle Paul gives this same counsel to Timothy when he says, "Do not rebuke an older man harshly, but exhort him as if he were your father. Treat younger men as brothers, older women as mothers, and younger women as sisters, with absolute purity" (II Timothy 5:1-2). The wisdom of this passage is that unless we grew up in a very dysfunctional family, we automatically know how to relate in love to our own family. If we can think of our flock as family members, older or younger, we will more likely treat them with love. Young pastors should not impose expectations on the older members of their flock that they would not impose on their parents or grandparents. The passage also speaks volumes about to how to relate to younger members of the flock as well.

Relate in the same way to all subcultures. It may take you a while to discern the different subcultures within the church, but they are there. At first, it appears there is just one congregation, but after a while it is evident that there are several. Some of the subcultures are related by blood, others by length of membership, others by age, socioeconomic, or ethnic factors. Some members pass easily from one group to the other, others keep close to their primary group. Even in very small churches, members of different groups often do not know each other. Frequently, there is a history of conflict among the groups that is discovered only in time. Each subculture will try to gain the pastor as an ally in support of their concerns. Be careful not to take sides but to treat everyone equally. In time, you may find a natural affinity and closeness toward one group, but even then be careful not to play favorites.

Seek your people's counsel. It simply makes sense to ask your people their ideas and feelings about what the church needs in order to be vital again. They have loved and served this church, sometimes their entire lives, so ask their opinions and then listen to them. You may not agree with their views; after all, the church has somehow reached this point of decline under their watch. But it is important that you hear their thoughts.

Learn the church's recent history. It can mean you can truthfully state, "We HAVE done it this way before," a counter to those most dreaded words, "We have NEVER done it this way before." Chances are that in the church's recent history there were some major efforts to evangelize the lost or to serve the poor and needy in the community. Learning that history means you can later leverage it to challenge the people to reach out again. Along with this, learn the town's history, and remind your people of who they are in the wider context. The church's recent history will tell you who your predecessors were, how they were received and why they left. It will tell you if the church is reacting to your immediate predecessor in their selection of you. If he or she was controlling, perhaps they assume you will be compliant. If he or she was passive, they may have chosen you in hopes you will be more directive. The recent history will also tell you about divisions in the church, what caused them and whether they have been healed. The recent history may also turn up a remnant of faithful, godly, praying members who have been waiting for someone to come and boldly proclaim the gospel. A remnant in a declined church is a wonderful gift from God. Throughout Israel's history, it was often for the sake of the remnant that God brought about revival. When Jesus sent out his disciples, he told them to look for the "man of peace" in a village, a sign that the gospel would be welcome there. It is a further confirmation of your call, that God has prepared, in advance, receptive soil for your ministry. Ironically, the remnant are usually not leaders but quiet, behind-the-scenes people who have been prayerfully awaiting your arrival.

Learn the church's distant history. Most churches are planted with a noble, godly vision in mind. What was that vision? Was it an evangelistic effort to reach a new part of the community? Was it a prayer society? A mission enterprise? What covenant with God did those founding members enter into? Sometimes a church can reclaim that founding vision and recast it for a new generation.

The church that I pastored was planted as an abolition church 15 years before the Civil War. The founder was a young Christian businessman who had witnessed a slave auction in Charleston, South Carolina. He was horrified by what he saw. Husbands and wives sold off separately, children wrenched from parents and sold. The raw evil of that event never left him. He was changed forever and vowed to God that some day he would do something about it. He moved to the North and formed an abolitionist prayer society that eventually grew into our church. We are thought to be the first church in American history to be founded on the issue of the abolition of slavery. Its members aided and abetted fugitive slaves as they made their way to freedom via the Underground Railroad. We were able to recapture that history as we sought to become a church that likewise cared for the least of the least in our community and in the wider world. Over time, our church became involved in such ministries as refugee resettlement, pregnancy care centers, homeless shelters, prison evangelism, and support for victims of human trafficking, children at risk, and missions in developing countries. We were able to leverage this great legacy by saying "We HAVE done it this way before."

Is there a stirring story related to the founding of your church? If so, recapture it, recast it, and use it to re-inspire. In Revelation 3, Jesus calls the dying church in Sardis to remember what they had received and heard from the Lord. Help your church remember its past.

Accept their traditions. It is so important that a pastor accept his or her new congregation on an "as is" basis, and that includes their traditions. Many of the church's traditions may seem odd, outmoded, exclusive, and therefore counterproductive to the renewal of the church. However, these traditions are what give meaning and a sense of belonging to the people. Long before you arrived on the scene, this congregation cared for and guided the church. Pastors have come and gone, but a core of lay leaders have to the best of their ability been stewards of the church, its property, its mission, and its traditions. Long before it was your church, it was their church. So, before you decide to jettison some seemingly outmoded program or tradition, take some time to understand where it came from and what its purpose was.

In my only full-time (35-year) pastorate, the church I served held an annual fall fair, whose sole purpose was to raise money to support the church. Church fairs were a huge part of New England church life then. While I had no problem with the fair, I had an ethical objection to the idea of a church selling goods to the community in order to pay the bills. I believed, and still do, that the congregation should support the ministry, not ask "the world" to do it. I also had a pastoral concern that the church fair took so much time and energy over the weeks leading up to it that no one had time to attend my bible study. I felt that the fair was "sucking all of the oxygen" out of my ministry. When I raised these concerns with the church leaders, I received strong pushback. I decided that if I could not fight them, I would join them. So I pitched in and helped out at the event.

In the process, I also learned about the origin of the fair. It had been started years earlier, mostly by retired women. Many had been factory workers who, now in their 70s, 80s, and 90s, were living on very small fixed incomes and little disposable income. But they did have time, and they did have skills in cooking, baking, sewing, knitting, and crafting. They took what they had and converted them into items that were then sold at the fair. In this way they helped support the church, and they clearly saw it as their ministry. They were glad that they could make up through this effort what they lacked in money to donate. The Lord showed me that I was using my theological correctness to take this ministry away from these dear saints. Had I persisted, I would have acted ignorantly, and without love. I would have robbed them of their opportunity to serve Christ and his church.

Over time, the fair diminished in size and participation as that older congregation passed on and as a younger, more affluent demographic came into the church and supported it through their giving. Eventually, the fair committee realized they could no longer carry on this tradition, and it died a quiet death. One Sunday morning soon afterward, we honored these faithful members who found a way to give to the church. I was so glad that I listened to the Holy Spirit and made the effort to understand this tradition.

Familiarize yourself with the church's documents. These include its bylaws, membership rules, covenant, statement of faith, and the like. In time, some of these documents may change, but for now, accept them and become conversant with them. These documents may be a tool that the Holy Spirit will use to help renew your church. They tell the story of who this church is and what its founding vision was. You can refer to the documents to remind your people who they (or their forebears) said they were. You can then lovingly say, "How about it?" and challenge them to live up to it. In this same way, the Reverend Doctor Martin Luther King, Jr., citing the words of the Declaration of Independence— "We hold these truths to be self-evident: that all men are created equal"—said to a racially divided America, "How about it? Do we believe that or not?" Don't underestimate the power of gently holding people accountable for their own words. Our young children use the same tactic against us: "You SAID we would . . . ."

Preach the gospel of grace. In the early days of a preaching ministry, it is vital to "keep the main thing the main thing." As young pastors, we often come into our first church preaching the sermons we preached in homiletics class at seminary, where we were preaching to our fellow students and our professors. If the congregation has experienced a time of division, or has slipped into legalism, or is just demoralized and tired, it needs the milk of the basic gospel message of God's love and grace in Christ Jesus.

Avoid arcane doctrines and obscure texts because, as any veteran pastor will tell you, your first 200 sermons are not going to be very good anyway. Stick with the basics, and use them to build up your congregation's confidence in Christ and their biblical memory and literacy.

Meet your neighbors and the "town fathers." Get out into the community and meet the other clergy, the city and school officials, and the merchants. Depending on the size of the community, they will already know of your arrival. But your meeting them on their turf will show your respect for them and your desire to be part of their community. It may be that no other clergy person has reached out to them; you may be the only pastor they will ever know. I became good friends with the town manager of the community in which our church was located. We often met for lunch, and a few years before he retired, he sought my counsel on knowing when it was time to retire. I was deeply honored to share with him my thoughts on how God guides us in discerning His will.

Assure your congregation that you plan to stay. No one knows the future, and God may call a pastor to leave a church after just a few years, but generally, longevity is needed to lead a church to renewal. One of the most important messages a pastor can convey to a congregation is his or her intention to stay. If the history of pastoral tenure has been one of short stays, it is likely that the congregation will assume your stay will also be brief. It is not surprising that churches are reluctant to embrace the changes a pastor wants to make if he or she will soon be leaving. As humans, we instinctively keep our distance from people we believe are going to be leaving us soon. This happens when someone is relocating far away or, sadly, when someone has a terminal illness. When we believe people are leaving us one way or another, we try to protect ourselves from the loss by pulling back from the relationship or by refusing to invest in the relationship in the first place. If you believe you have been called to the ministry of revitalization, trust that God will keep you there as long as is needed to lead the church back to vitality, and convey that message to your flock. Stay at your post, until God clearly leads you on. I'll say more about this in a later chapter.

One of the organizations with which Overseed partners is a fellowship of revitalization pastors in northern New England called "25 To Life" (http://www.25tolifeforjesus.com). The name is clever, but the mission is a serious attempt to support and encourage pastors to stay faithful for the long haul so that fruit is born, communities are transformed, and Christ is honored.

There are ministries a pastor can undertake in this season that will begin to build a foundation for the next. A pastor can and should start a small group Bible study for any who want to attend, but especially for leaders. Or a pastor can introduce an Alpha course and encourage his leaders to attend. These kinds of ministries do not significantly impact the church's budget, and in a small church the pastor can provide all the leadership needed.

Pray for Your People. I found it helpful to sometimes slip into the sanctuary on a Saturday night and, with the lights low, visualize my people seated in their pews. I would then simply pray for them, and for me, that I might be a faithful servant of the word in the service the next morning.

. . . . .

To sum up, the honeymoon is a time for waiting on God and listening to your people and to the Holy Spirit. It is a time for you to learn about your people, who they are, where they have come from, where God is leading them. It is a time for you to hear the stories they have longed to tell a shepherd who will listen.

It is also a time for you to tell the congregation who you are and what your life and faith journey has been. Share with your people what God is saying to you. Become oriented to the larger community that has hosted and shaped your congregation, perhaps for hundreds of years. And as you seek to build that foundation of trust, you would do well to heed the advice of the gifted Bible teacher and pastor Earl Palmer: Pay your dues. Palmer spoke of four types of dues a pastor owes his or her congregation. Your people want to know that (1) you are working hard; (2) you are growing; (3) you love the Lord; and (4) you love them. Be diligent in paying those dues. Above all, love your people sincerely with the love God pours into your heart.

5

Avoiding Pitfalls

The Honeymoon Season is a reservoir of good will and grace given to you by the congregation. Build that supply by responding with love, patience, and acceptance. The time will come when you will need to draw down that reserve as you lead change. In the meantime, avoid making these mistakes that may jeopardize or tarnish the honeymoon.

Do not make any major changes. In the Honeymoon Season of the first one to two years, do not make any major changes unless the congregation is asking you to make them. Especially, do not significantly modify the worship service. It is hard to resist the urge to make changes in the early going. In a declining church, there may be much that needs to change if it is to be renewed. As I stated in the previous chapter, I believe the single greatest mistake young, inexperienced pastors make is to introduce major change before they have earned the trust and support of the congregation. Often it is a fatal mistake for the pastor and sometimes for the congregation. And it is not just a rookie mistake; many a veteran pastor has shipwrecked a promising ministry by moving too fast too soon. You must have confidence in your calling and in His timing. You must have faith in the people who called you. Believe that they also are listening to God and, given good reason and enough time, will embrace change.

Part of the ministry of Overseed is to lead conferences for young replant pastors and their wives. A young pastor and his wife attended a recent conference. They had been at their church for just a couple of years but had already introduced major changes. As I spoke about the need to move slowly in changing worship, it was evident by his questions that this young pastor was concerned that he had moved too fast. He interrupted my talk several times to describe the changes he had made. He asked if I thought he had made a mistake and if it was too late for him to regain the congregation's trust and support. I tried to reassure him that it was not too late, prayed with him and his wife, and gave them some ideas on how he might proceed to correct the course. A few months later I learned the outcome. When they returned from vacation that summer, he was asked to resign. He, his wife, and their young child were given two months to find a new call and vacate the parsonage. He was devastated. It had indeed been too late. I only wish we had been able to talk to him a couple of years earlier and urge him to see the honeymoon season as an opportunity from God to go slow and build trust.

Do not arrive with a ready-made vision. Vision is vital in a replant ministry, or any important leadership role. It takes a clearly seen and articulated vision of ministry to lead a declining church to renewal. But that vision is not something the pastor formulates beforehand and brings to the church on day one. It must take shape gradually in the shepherd's mind and heart. Vision by its nature has specificity. Vision is for a particular people, in a particular place, for a particular time. It is hoped that a vision will develop in your mind over time as you listen to God and to the

44

people you are called to serve. Never be in a hurry with vision; it will emerge in time. When it does, it will make sense to the congregation and to the surrounding community since it is divine in origin. It will be unique to your setting, which is why vision cannot be borrowed from another church and superimposed on yours. Moreover, God rarely, if ever, gives a vision to a committee. At least since the time of Moses, God has spoken in mass to His people through one individual. He continues to do that. As pastor, you are that individual.

Do not criticize the past. It is tempting for new pastors to focus on all the negatives they've inherited. It may be obvious how your church has suffered from a lack of effective pastoral leadership or how the people have made poor decisions. So many of the churches in America are in a woebegone state due to theological drift away from biblical, historical Christian orthodoxy. If it is not theological drift, it is missional shift as a church moves into a club member mentality, concerned only about itself and not the thousands of people who are living and dying within the church's shadow. Righteous anger is an appropriate response for a pastor surveying the neglect of previous shepherds. In this early season, though, it is neither helpful nor fair to criticize the previous leaders and the decisions they made. It is not helpful because it is too late, the decisions of the past have been made, and by criticizing them, you are criticizing the people in your church who were part of those decisions. It is not fair because you do not know all of the reasons for the decisions. Honeymoon pastors must remember that they are now in their congregations' HOME, and until they have stayed long enough to make it *their own* home, criticism of the past is counterproductive.

When I arrived at the church that I served for 35 years, it was somewhat divided over the previous pastor. He had stayed only 5 years and was then forced into early retirement by the unrelenting criticism of some of the younger members of the church. He had succeeded during his 5 years in driving many of the younger families out of the church with his policies that favored the older congregation. When I arrived, I listened to both sides of the story. Being young myself, I tended to believe the tales of the younger families, especially how he had forced out a popular youth minister as well as a popular music director. I refrained from publically criticizing him even though in my mind I was definitely blaming him. Over the next few years, some facts emerged about both the former ousted staff members. The local newspaper reported that the youth minister was arrested, tried, convicted, and sentenced following a long pattern of violent physical abuse of his wife and children. The marriage ended, and the wife came back to our church and has been a faithful member ever since. Not long after that, the former music director was arrested and convicted of sexual assault and indecency. I do not know the circumstances that led to the firing of these two staff members, but evidently my predecessor knew something of their true characters. He realized they had no place in the church's ministry. My respect for my predecessor increased dramatically. I thanked God that he had done the difficult and costly work of removing from the Body of Christ these ministers who had so egregiously violated their holy calling. I realized I had been unfairly judging him and that I should have kept an open mind about him. I later had the opportunity to meet him and thank him for his ministry.

Do not dwell on numbers. Easier said than done. As pastors, we love to measure our success in terms of Sunday morning attendance. We seem to be obsessed with numbers. We constantly check our attendance figures trying to reassure ourselves of the success of our ministry. Is it not true that one of the first questions pastors asks each other when they meet is "How big is your congregation?" I cannot think of any other profession where people ask that of their colleagues. Do medical doctors ask one another, "How big is your practice?" or lawyers, "How many clients do you have?" It is probably a measure of our insecurity that we almost immediately ask this question of our colleagues. If it turns out that our colleague's church is larger than ours, we feel discouraged. On the other hand, if his or her church is smaller, we feel superior. The problem with the question is that no two churches are the same. Individual churches are incomparable. Early on, I was too concerned about attendance figures and would check the ushers' figures as soon as the service was over. If the number was higher than I expected, I felt elated and a little prideful. If the number was lower than I expected, I felt discouraged and questioned my leadership ability. Sometimes, if the number was really low, I would feel mildly depressed well into my day off on Monday. It was too much, so I decided to stop looking at the attendance register and just focus on being the most faithful pastor I could be. For years, I had little idea of what the numbers actually were, but determined to minister to whoever showed up. I was a lot happier, and I enjoyed my day off a lot more.

Plainly, it is important for churches to keep a record of the attendance because numbers are important. They show healthy or unhealthy trends in the life of a church. Each of the numbers represents a person made in the image of God and precious to him. The numbers are not cold statistics. They do tell a story. When a pastor or a congregation says they do not want to "play the numbers game," it may be a cover for the fact that the numbers are not good. It is important for a pastor to know what the attendance trend is over time. However, it is better to focus on leading the church to greater spiritual health and to trust God to "give the increase." It is common for attendance numbers to decline in the first year or two of a pastor's ministry as existing members evaluate the new pastor and make a decision to stay or go elsewhere. (And going elsewhere is certainly better than staying and opposing the pastor's leadership.) Remember, not all forms of growth are good: even cemeteries grow, but with dead people.

Do not focus on those who leave. No doubt some people will leave during the honeymoon. When they do, follow up with a phone call or a visit to try to find out why. Realize that rarely will people who are leaving tell you why. However, it is important to ask because you may learn from it. Make a sincere effort to get them to reconsider, knowing that it is unlikely they will change their mind. When you are sure that they have made up their minds, then let them go with your blessing. One of the ways our enemy discourages us is to focus our attention on the people who are leaving and not on the people who are staying.

Some of the best advice I ever received in this regard was during my early years as a youth minister with the Young Life ministry. We had a large, vibrant high school Young Life ministry, with many new kids showing up each week to our Club meeting (the outreach ministry of Young Life). But many others were going out the back door just as fast. When I ran into kids around town who were no longer attending the Club meetings, I would become discouraged and wonder why I was failing. When I shared this with my Young Life supervisor, he said, "Why don't you focus on the kids you have and not worry about those you don't have?" Such simple but sound advice. Usually, there is little we can do once a person has decided to leave. Now, there may be a pattern in why people are leaving, and that *is* important to know. But if that is not the case, then trust that God knows what he is doing, and put your attention on those who are staying.

Avoid Sunday surprises. Do not make your congregation anxious on Sunday mornings! You don't want them coming to church wondering what changes you've made or what issues you'll address. Your motto should be the same as Holiday Inn's: "The Best Surprise is NO SURPRISE." Be sure to prepare the congregation for any changes you do plan to make, even if it prolongs the process. Your congregation is a captive audience and your sermon is a monologue, so do not put them on edge with unexpected tweaks or controversial topics. They are still getting to know you, and they want to be able to trust you. With that in mind, preach the word faithfully and let God's word do the work of convicting and transforming. If your congregation can trust you in the pulpit, they will trust you in the committee meetings.

Do not develop a "me and them" attitude. Your congregation may not be as spiritually mature as you want them to be, but they are the flock God has given you, not your enemies. The Apostle Paul is our example in how he addressed the Corinthian congregation. We know of the problems and failings of that people, yet Paul called them "the church of God . . . those sanctified in Christ Jesus, and called to be holy . . . ." They were sanctified, but still in need of greater holiness. That is who your people are. Accept them, and disciple everyone who responds regardless of where you think they are spiritually. If they show up on Sunday mornings or at a Bible study, work with them. We are tempted to divide people into our categories of spiritual maturity based on what we see, but God sees the heart.

This was another valuable lesson I learned in Young Life. At one point in my youth ministry, I recall three freshman boys attending the Young Life Club. They were socially immature, always clowning around, showing little interest in the Christian message. I tended to overlook them, assuming they were not interested and not listening. However, they *were* listening, and the Holy Spirit was speaking to them. When they started attending Campaigners (the small group discipleship component of Young Life), I didn't know what to do with them. I had pegged them as not spiritually mature enough to be there. My Young Life advisor cautioned, "They are there for a reason—just disciple them." I did. All three boys gave their lives to Christ and grew in their faith. Years later, two had become foreign missionaries, taking the gospel to the jungles of Brazil and Muslim Europe, respectively. The third is a senior lay leader in a young, dynamic, rapidly growing church plant in New England. God taught the prophet Samuel the same lesson when he almost overlooked young David as King of Israel: "Men look at the outward things, but God looks at the heart."

Do not dwell on financial matters. Let the congregation handle the money. You put your effort into discerning the mission and vision of the church. The church may be in financial straits; if so, trust God's promise to meet the church's needs. When the church leadership realizes that you are trusting them to steward the resources, they will live up to that trust. In time, you will have opportunities to teach biblical stewardship, but during the honeymoon, let them worry about the money.

Do not expect the church to conform to you. Instead, you conform to their culture. The time will come when pastor and congregation will be called to conform more and more to Christ, but initially, as a good missionary, be sensitive to the culture God has called you to and minister within their expectations.

· · · · ·

My wife and I have four-year-old twin grandchildren. They are endlessly curious, constantly exploring, looking at everything, asking what it is and why it is there. To paraphrase our Lord, "Lest you become as a four-year-old, ye shall in no wise build trust during the honeymoon." Find out what your church does, and why. Until you know that, hands off.

In this Honeymoon Season, you are asking your people to "loan" authority to you, to trust you on a trial basis, until you have proven trustworthy and earned the authority to lead them. Have confidence that over time your authority will accrue, but for now go slowly and earn the right to lead by loving your people and believing God.

6

Catalyzing Change

In a marriage, a couple typically comes back from the honeymoon—that time of celebration and discovery and growing trust—and settles into the business of life. They return to jobs, responsibilities, creating a household, making plans, and moving forward with those plans. In these early years of marriage, however, many couples find they have brought very different expectations into the relationship. They experience real conflict for the first time. This can also describe the early years of ministry. Following the honeymoon, a congregation and pastor begin to experience conflict as they realize they, too, have brought very different expectations into their "marriage." As they get down to the routine business of church life, the conflict begins.

It is in these years following the honeymoon that replant pastors recognize and exercise their dual role as chaplain/catalyst. The role of chaplain continues as they care for the flock God has given them, but the role of catalyst begins as they also challenge the congregation to discover God's plans for the church. This is the scenario for the beginning of conflict.

Even though a pastor and congregation were intentional in the "engagement" season and patient in the "honeymoon" season, conflict is almost inevitable in the third season of leading change. This is a season of trying to understand one another's expectations and to discern the way forward. No matter how intentional a pastor is during the honeymoon, conflict is likely to emerge—or erupt—in the third season of a ministry: the season of catalyzing and then leading change.

Andy Stanley rightly observes that every church is perfectly engineered to get exactly the result it is getting. A church in need of renewal, however, wants a different future. Maybe they want to grow, or to get younger, or to reach their community for Christ. In each case, the path to that different future involves change. We all know the definition of *insanity* is "doing the same thing over and over but expecting different results." This is one of those profound truisms that so many pastors have heard but fail to fully understand and appreciate. Because no one likes change and the conflict that inevitably comes with it, we hope that somehow we can achieve a new future without doing anything different. It can't be done.

Change is essential if an organism or an organization is to remain healthy and live. As long as we simply maintain the status quo, our church will continue to decline and eventually die. In fact, not only will it not grow, it won't even stay the same—it will go backward. G. K. Chesterton summed up the paradox this way: "In order to stay the same, you have to change."

THE PATIENT CHAPLAIN

Some pastors are simply not change agents but are very comfortable in the role of chaplain. There is a place for a chaplain in ministry if the congregation has simply decided to die. In that case, the pastor helps prepare them for that inevitability. The statistics for churches choosing to die over the next few decades are staggering and alarming. According to Thom Rainer, somewhere between 7,000 and 10,000 churches in America will close their doors in the next year (Blog, "Growing Healthy Churches, Together," 6-12-17). The fact is, not all churches can be renewed; some churches will simply die.

If a church has decided to die, then a pastor can help it die with dignity, and there are steps a church can take to do so. It can give its building and assets to a vital church in the community that has a reasonable chance to repopulate it and lead it in a new direction. It can sell its property and give the proceeds to the denomination to which it belongs. Some denominations have an active process to this end, sometimes called a "legacy" church program, in which the assets of a dying church are used to plant new churches. A dying church can merge with a healthier church in the community that shares some of the same theology and values. Of course, in a merger the weaker church, over time, will almost certainly cease to exist. A dying church can give or sell the church building to the local community as a community center, library, town office, low-income or senior housing, or for some other purpose that will benefit those in the community. The death of a church is not a pleasant thing, but if that is what a congregation has chosen, then a chaplain pastor can help guide the process toward a purposeful termination.

There are no doubt other reasons why a pastor might choose the role of chaplain over change agent. One reason might be that he or she is near enough to retirement that risking the possibility of losing the job is unthinkable. While this is understandable from a human point of view, it is unfortunate from a kingdom perspective.

Another reason for a pastor choosing to remain as a chaplain is that he or she simply does not have the personality and spiritual gifts needed to deal with conflict. While almost no one likes conflict, there are people who avoid it like the plague. A pastor whose personality leads him or her to avoid conflict at all costs will find it extremely difficult to lead the change necessary to see the church renewed.

However, if a pastor is called to replant a church, then in this third season of the process he or she will begin to intentionally shift from chaplain to change agent, or catalyzer. It is this dual role of "chaplain/change agent" or "patient catalyst" that makes church revitalization so challenging. A pastor must be both at the same time. It's not unlike walking a tightrope. The natural tendency is to err on one side or the other. But leaning too much either way has consequences. Staying in chaplain mode too long may result in the window for leading change narrowing or even closing. In my experience if a pastor has not begun to bring significant change within this period, from year 3 to 6 of a pastorate, then he or she will face stronger resistance when change finally is introduced. I'm reminded of a pastor who served a small church in coastal Maine. For years, he simply tried to be their chaplain. Then, when he did try to lead the church forward in mission to the local community, he got such opposition that he had to leave. One elderly deacon expressed the sentiment of the congregation when he said to my friend, as only a Mainer can say, "Pastor, when you first came here, you said you liked us the way we were. Now, you want to go and change us all around." Don't wait too long to shift to catalyst.

On the other hand, if you move to bring about change too quickly (and this is more likely), then you will probably provoke a strong pushback from the congregation, which will make leading change very difficult. Finding that right balance of "patient catalyst" is what makes church revitalization so demanding. Let's look at what it takes to shift from chaplain to change agent.

THE CATALYZING CHANGE AGENT

The replant pastor *must* be a change agent, initiating and leading change. If this is not in your DNA as a pastor, then replanting is not for you. The call is all about leading change. Without change, a declining church will continue on its slide to further decline and eventual death. Not surprisingly, it takes a leader to lead change. My thoughts on leadership are short and simple.

First, I believe that leadership is a spiritual gift that God gives to pastors. In Romans 12:8, Paul says that if one's "gift is leadership, then let him lead diligently." We know that spiritual gifts are the dynamic equipping that God gives to all believers to enable them to serve the greater Body of Christ. As shepherds of a flock, pastors should assume that, as part of their calling, they have the gift of leadership and therefore should lead.

Second, I believe that leaders are made, not born. Leadership is not an innate or instinctual talent. Although there are certain personality characteristics that may lend themselves to leadership, I think we often confuse a strong personality with effective leadership. A pastor who does not naturally have a forceful, persuasive personality may feel he or she is not able to be a leader. Strong personalities are often very polarizing. People either like them or not. So strong personalities may *not* make the most effective leaders.

Third, there are many types of effective leaders. No two people are alike, so rather than try to imitate someone else's style, develop your own. Some of the most effective leaders I have known have been very quiet, even shy-appearing men and women of God, but they loved their people, prayed faithfully and earnestly, believed that God had called them to lead their church forward into new life. Do not count yourself out as a leader just because you don't fit into some preconceived image.

Edwin Friedman has a helpful discussion of leadership styles in his book *Generation to Generation*. He points out that leadership style is like two poles at opposite ends of a spectrum. On one end is the charismatic leader, and on the other is the consensus-building leader. Almost all discourse about leadership is based on this continuum. In the 1960s and 1970s, the consensus-building model was in vogue in Christian circles, whereas by the 1980s and 1990s, the model of the charismatic leader pastoring the attractional church was the fashion. Both models are problematic.

The problem with the charismatic leader model is that it is a rare gift. There are in fact very few charismatic leaders in any population, clergy or otherwise. For the pastor who is not charismatic (the vast majority of us), the assumption is that you will not be an effective leader. Worse, you may try to fake the charismatic style with a forced, boisterous personality. This is easily seen as insincere and is off-putting.

The problem with the consensus-building model is that it is very inefficient in terms of both time and energy expended by the pastor. Unless the consensus sought is among a very small group of people, the outcome will be a watered-down, compromised effort aimed to please everyone.

As Friedman notes, this polarity view of leadership has even more serious problems. For instance, the charismatic person's leadership can be polarizing. People tend to either like or dislike the charismatic person. Those who like the person, like him strongly, but those who dislike the person strongly dislike him. The issues involved in leading a church get wrapped up in the leader's personality. Opposition and disagreement are felt to be "personal." Charismatic leaders are also required always to be "on," always functioning at a high energy level. They must constantly act strong, exuding the confidence and enthusiasm that draws people to them. No one can continuously function at a high level, so a false persona is developed. One final problem with the charismatic leader is that there is never an easy succession plan. When the leader goes, the power and effectiveness go, too, and the church is left without a leader.

The problem with the consensus-building model, Friedman points out, is that a group does not receive a "call." It has always been individuals, not committees, who hear the voice of God and receive the vision. It was to Moses, not to the Israelites, that God spoke directly on Mt. Sinai. God speaks to individuals, and the individual must then speak to the group in such a way that the group is freely persuaded to follow. The vision is not commanded, but cast, so that others see it. Unfortunately, some churches try to develop a vision through a group process. They form "vision committees" or "dream teams." This process can help flesh out a vision after the fact, but rarely can it provide the vision. This notion of group vision and leadership runs strong in declined churches because they have had to function without pastoral leadership. The pastor may be told he is "just one vote," or as is common in congregationally governed churches, he may not even get a vote at all. Another problem with the consensus model is that Individuals can hold a group process hostage to get their way. The result is a watered-down vision and bogged-down activity that inspires no one and moves the church nowhere. Pastors are shepherds and the shepherd must lead the sheep, not the other way around.

Because both poles on this continuum of charismatic and consensus leadership are fraught with problems, we need a different understanding of leadership. A better way is to think of leaders as people who have a strong, healthy sense of who they are and of their divine calling. So whatever their personality type, whether extroverted or introverted, is irrelevant if they are self-aware and secure in their call. Friedman's term for this state is "self-differentiated." It is essentially knowing who you are with all of your strengths and weaknesses and being comfortable with it. I believe that a self-differentiated sense of self-acceptance is born out of God's acceptance of you in Christ. When pastors function out of that sense of self-acceptance, and confidence in God's acceptance, they are freer and more effective as leaders. They are less likely to be controlled or intimidated by outside forces or personalities.

RESISTANCE TO CHANGE

In many churches that need replanting, it is not uncommon for the pastor's role to be seen as that of "follower of the sheep," not leader of the sheep. This is understandable since the congregation itself has assumed the leadership role in the church. After all, they have been the constant factor in the church as pastors have come and gone. This is especially true in churches that have had consistently short pastoral tenures. Those congregations are reluctant to surrender leadership to the pastor since they figure he or she will probably not be staying long. It is the lay people in small, declining churches who know how to keep the institution functioning. They know how to prepare the annual budget and collect the pledges. They know how to run the fund-raising programs, maintain the church's property, and manage its investments. They know how to nominate people to fill the operating committees. They know the church year and how to prepare the music and liturgy for the various holidays. They can provide worship leaders and, if needed, can even preach a sermon. They know the needs of the congregation—who is hospitalized, unemployed, out of sorts with the church, and so on. In a limited way, they can provide for the pastoral needs of the congregation.

This church can typically function just fine for a while without a pastor. Why are we surprised that the notion of the pastor leading change is resisted? Church lay leaders will often firmly believe that they are capable of leading the church forward. However, common sense and experience tell us that a group cannot lead change. As we will explore later, there is a place for what John Kotter calls a "guiding coalition" that will help inform, implement, and institutionalize the change. But the pastor must take the lead. He or she must not surrender this role to a committee. Plainly, if the church were capable of leading change without the pastor, it would not be in decline and in need of revitalization. It is because of a lack of leadership introducing and guiding change that a church has arrived where it is.

New Wine in New Wineskins

When you begin to introduce change in a church, you may be astonished by how fierce the resistance is. In your mind, a change may seem very minor, and so the intensity of the opposition may catch you off-guard. It is interesting that the very first parable Jesus tells in the Gospel of Luke deals with change and people's reaction to it. It is often called the "Parable of the Wine Skins" (Luke 5:36-39).

> He told them this parable: "No one tears a patch from a new garment and sews it on an old one. If he does, he will have torn the new garment, and the patch from the new will not match the old. And no one pours new wine into old wineskins. If he does, the new wine will burst the skins, the wine will run out and the wineskins will be ruined. No, new wine must be poured into new wineskins. And no one after drinking old wine wants the new, for he says, 'the old is better.'"

I had preached on this text many times before really noticing the ending of the parable and what may be its most practical lesson. I think Jesus's key point in this story of new and old cloth, new and old wineskins, is that the message that He was bringing was not going to be a revision of the old. It was going to be something entirely new. Jesus's message was not a reform message. It was not like the message of the prophets, calling Israel back again and again to God. It was not like the message of the Pharisees or even the message of John the Baptist, the last of the Old Covenant prophets. Jesus's message was radically new, and the parable was teaching this. The truth of the Gospel would not simply be a patch on the garment of the Old Covenant; it would be the new garment of the New Covenant. The same message is conveyed using the image of the wine skins. To take Jesus any other way, the parable says, would be destructive. He is saying that his teaching has to be received as something totally new. While the Gospel had been foretold in the Old Testament, it was not to be received as a new patch repairing a flaw in the old. It was and is completely new, and Jesus Christ had to be newly received by each person.

That is how I understood and preached this passage over the years. In the Gospel, God is doing a new thing. It was much later, as I personally experienced fierce resistance to my leadership in a small rural church I pastored briefly in retirement, that I noticed the ending of the parable. And it hit home.

The last verse of the parable (verse 39), although somewhat enigmatic, is actually profound. It is a surprise ending to the story. One would expect Jesus to say that once people have tasted the "new wine" of the Gospel, no one will want to go back to the old wine of the Law. That would make sense because it is true. Once people discover the living truth of Jesus Christ and all that it brings, no one would want to go back to the empty forms of religion. But that's not what He says. In fact, He says just the opposite: that once people drink the new wine, they will desire the old wine, thinking it is better.

Here is the simple meaning of the end of the parable: Because the Gospel is radical, it is unfamiliar, perhaps scary, and for some, anyway, hard to fully embrace. Isn't it true that discovering Jesus Christ often produces at least a momentary hesitation or holding back from full commitment because of His sweeping and life-changing claims? The parable also predicts the wholesale rejection Jesus knows will come from Ancient Israel.

For those of us who are striving to lead the hard change of church revitalization, these words of Jesus are encouraging. We should expect that when our church members taste the new wine we are introducing, they will impulsively reject it in favor of the familiar flavor of the old. The parable of the wineskins is very instructive for the replant pastor. Jesus is declaring that no one likes change and that, given a choice, people will invariably reject the new in favor of the old. Every pastor who wants to see his or her church renewed should prayerfully listen to this warning from our Lord. Over time, however, even the unfamiliar "new" wine will season gracefully and become a fine vintage that blesses for generations to come.

I firmly believe that the most difficult obstacle a pastor has to deal with when seeking to lead church renewal is resistance to change. A replant pastor must lead change, and yet that effort will most certainly result in resistance and often conflict. It is often at this point that a pastor in a replant church gets into trouble. Sometimes the resistance is so fierce that the pastor ends up leaving in discouragement or frustration. Too many promising pastoral careers have been cut short by the painful experience of heels dug in against pastoral leadership. This is especially true when the resistance is unexpected, and a pastor feels completely blindsided by it. I try to tell pastors to *expect* resistance and conflict. If you expect it, then you have begun the process of dealing with it. (In Chapter 8, we'll examine ways to minimize and manage conflict.)

The Climate for Change

Knowing that forewarned is forearmed, I recommend Lyle Schaller *Strategies for Change*. It contains an excellent chapter on discerning the climate for change in a church. That is, are the conditions conducive to change or not? The answer has a lot to do with the starting point of the church in the revitalization process. If your predecessor has introduced change in a healthy way and has brought the church forward in its mission, then the climate for further change will be positive. On the other hand, some factors negatively impact the climate for change. Schaller's categories—adversarial, apathetic, complacent, and energized—may be helpful as you forecast the climate for change in your particular church.

1. ***Adversarial.*** Is there unresolved conflict in the church between factions or with a former pastor? Is there conflict between the current pastor and staff members? Schaller strongly recommends healing the conflict before you move on with introducing change. It is easier to lead a healthy church forward. You need to heal before you can grow.

2. ***Apathetic.*** Is the participation rate low? Is the membership aging and in sharp decline? Do people leave right after worship services? Is it difficult to recruit volunteers? Do the leaders fail to participate in the life of the church? If the answer to these questions is yes, it will probably be very difficult to lead change. A church like this probably does not have the strength to survive the trauma associated with change. The average age of the congregation will definitely be a factor. Older congregations may have a sense that they have served their time and now want to spend their remaining years traveling or with grandchildren. In this climate, there is little energy for the change needed for renewal.

3. ***Complacent.*** Is everyone relatively content with the status quo? Are attendance and giving strong enough to make it seem as if the church is healthy? Year after year, are the budgets met and the committees filled? In such a church, there is often a sense of community among the insiders, but it rarely extends to newcomers. There is no felt need to change anything. The church "feels" alive, but it is probably already carrying the seeds of its own demise. This church bears a strong resemblance to the church in Sardis, in Asia Minor, that Jesus addressed in Revelation 3:1–2: "I know your deeds; you have a reputation of being alive, but you are dead. Wake up! Strengthen what remains and is about to die . . . ." Complacency is probably the most difficult climate for revitalization because there is

the illusion of life and health and therefore no felt need to change.

4. ***Energized.*** Is attendance increasing? Is there openness to newcomers? Is conflict minimal and spiritual growth evident? In this setting, the climate for change is excellent. Perhaps the previous pastor or an interim pastor has already done some of the hard work of renewal to create this climate. Perhaps the church has experienced a spiritual revival among some of the older leaders, or an influx of believers from another congregation, and change is happening organically. In an energized church, there is usually a good match—and the likelihood of a long-term relationship—between the pastor and congregation. There is less concern about continuity with the past and more interest in the future. This is a description of a church that can be said to be in the process of revitalization.

The human reaction to change is well explained by Friedman in *Generation to Generation.* He uses the psychological term *homeostasis* to describe the state of equilibrium that all living organisms seek. When change is introduced, homeostasis is disrupted and the organism fights with all its resources to reestablish balance. Don't underestimate how powerful a force homeostasis is. Consider the fact that, before your arrival, your church spent years or even decades establishing routines, traditions, and patterns of activity that enable it to function. It may not be functioning well. In fact, it may be quite dysfunctional. Even that very dysfunction is the homeostasis that enables it to survive. The dysfunction is its normal. If you ask the people in a church that is in dire need of revitalization, they will say they need to grow or to attract younger families or to truly serve their communities. They may even admit they need to change. Yet when you begin to introduce the very change they say they want and need, be prepared for resistance

63

because you have upset the homeostasis of the congregation. It's virtually inevitable.

Remember the honeymoon season? During the honeymoon you came to appreciate the huge investment the church has in its traditions and routines. Ideally, you built up a stock of trust with your patience. That reservoir will be rapidly paid down in the season of change, when you transition from chaplain to catalyst.

7

Leading Change

One of the most popular and insightful books on leading change has that very title: *Leading Change*, by Harvard University Professor Emeritus John Kotter. I recommend that every replant pastor give it a thorough reading. Professor Kotter's research and conclusions about leading change in the corporate world largely apply to the local church as well. Perhaps the reason why the process of leading change is similar in both corporate and church settings is that both are family systems, and so the human dynamics are very much alike. In both settings, there is tremendous resistance to change by either company employees or church members. Many a chief executive and many a pastor fail to lead the change needed because they do not fully understand and appreciate the dynamics of change and the process of leading it.

Leaders have been successfully leading change in churches and other contexts for centuries without the assistance of modern sociology because many leaders are intuitive, discerning, persuasive, and patient. Long before road maps and GPS, people found their way; but road maps and GPS make it easier. In the same way, Kotter's insights constitute a useful road map for helping us navigate the dynamics of the change process.

I have taken the liberty of adapting Kotter's eight principles of leading change, focusing on the first four as they are the most critical in a church setting and so warrant the most attention here. The last four are compressed in this discussion as being no less strategic but more easily achieved once the hard work of the first four is done.

ESTABLISHING A SENSE OF URGENCY

When a pastor is called to a church in need of revitalization, it is a matter of life or death for that church. The church is on a path toward demise. That death may be soon or it may be decades away. A hefty endowment or careful management of resources enables some declined churches to stay open indefinitely with few members. Declined churches have an uncanny will to live. In my work with Overseed in New England, I have encountered congregations with fewer than ten active members and yet they find a way to live on. Death, though, is on the horizon. You may be familiar with Dr. Elizabeth Kubler-Ross, the Swiss-American psychiatrist whose pioneering studies of grief and death resulted in her classic *On Death and Dying*. Kubler-Ross determined that the first stage of dying is **denial.** Many churches in need of revitalization are in a state of denial. That denial reinforces the homeostasis that they struggle to maintain. Often there is no sense of the urgency of the church's condition. As a replant pastor, you must help your flock face reality and gain a sense of urgency about their future. You must help them face the fact that unless something changes, they will continue to decline and eventually die.

Just as with treating physical illness, sometimes the cure seems worse than the disease. Some people and some churches reach the point where the treatment to get better is more painful than dying. There are churches in which it is easier for an elderly and tired congregation to die than to change. As noted in Chapter 3, discerning this attitude should be part of the engagement season. As pastors, we may be willing to sacrifice our lives for the sake of Christ, but none of us has time to waste attempting renewal where there is no will.

However, if you discern that there is a will to live, then as you get to know your congregation, you will be able to sense what it is that will foster a sense of urgency. You will prayerfully discern what will motivate the church to undertake the effort necessary for a transformation to happen.

Initially, the sense of urgency may arise simply from the need to pay the bills to keep the church open. While it may not be a noble reason, if it moves the congregation to consider changing in order to live again, then it is a starting point in the renewal process. Similarly, the urgency may come from a desire to repair the church building. There is often idolatry about church buildings. It may be that the building is historic, or that the current members' forebears built the church, or that the structure is a landmark in the community. Again, it may not be a very spiritual beginning, but if the congregation has a strong desire to maintain or improve the building, the pastor should embrace that. The building, after all, is the repository of tender memories for the people. It is sacred space that at one point in history was set apart as holy ground for God's purposes. It is a symbol of their faithfulness that could be the starting point for creating a sense of urgency. A wise pastor will not quickly dismiss this as a motivation for renewal.

A more biblical starting point for creating a sense of urgency might be for the congregation to desire to reach a certain segment of the population. For example, if the congregation is mostly women, then the urgency might be to reach the husbands of these women. As farfetched as that may sound, I am very familiar with an American Baptist Church in which this was the case. The congregation had dwindled to about 40 on a Sunday, mostly middle-aged and older women. They called a dynamic young pastor and his wife and prayed with him that he would lead the church to try to reach their husbands and their sons. This young pastor determined that many of the husbands and sons were motorcycle enthusiasts, and so he bought a motorcycle, learned to ride it, and began reaching out to the men on the fringes of the church. He became the chaplain of a local motorcycle group, and today, 12 years later, the church numbers about 250 in attendance with many younger families. Many of the men in leadership positions are motorcycle riders whom he led to Christ. Of course, there were other factors that led to the renewal of this congregation, including practical biblical preaching, inspiring worship, united prayer by the congregation, evangelism, and definitely perseverance. But the sense of urgency was established with a desire on the part of prayerful women to enfold their husbands and sons in the church and the kingdom.

The sense of urgency may also be found in a church's desire to reach its community for Christ. In churches with a history of evangelism and mission, this may be the point of urgency. If the congregation is made up of people who were themselves won to Christ in an evangelistic movement, they may have the zeal to reach their families and friends if an effective means— such as Alpha—is deployed. As pastor, you may have the gift of evangelism and can lead this effort yourself. But if you don't, look for some leader(s) who do and nurture and support them to take the leadership role in evangelism. The memory of souls won to Christ in the past may be the impetus needed to initiate change.

One of the most natural ways to create a sense of urgency in a declining and dying church is to tap into the longing of Christian parents and grandparents to see their children and grandchildren won to Christ. So many of the Psalms speak eloquently of the longing to see the next generation know the Lord. For example, Psalm 71:18, "Even when I am old and gray, do not forsake me, O

God, till I declare your power to the next generation...." Or Psalm 78:3-4, " . . . what we have heard and known, what our fathers have told us. We will not hide them from their children, we will tell the next generation the praiseworthy deeds of the Lord...." Other Psalms that speak of this longing include Ps. 22:30-31; 78:6; 79:13; 89:1; 102:18; and 145:4. The old gospel song's question, "Will the circle be unbroken by and by?" expresses the profound hope that one day we will be gathered to glory with our family intact. If the children and grandchildren of the members actually reside nearby, then this may be the most powerful starting point in creating a sense of urgency in a local congregation.

Even if your members' children do not live nearby and are not likely ever to be won by your church, you can begin to urgently pray for their children and grandchildren, that they will be won to Christ by churches in the places where they live. Then you can challenge them to seek to win their children's generation who *do* reside locally. Encourage them to think of themselves as spiritual parents and grandparents. The Apostle John speaks of spiritual fathers, and Paul speaks of both spiritual fathers and mothers. You can tap into the natural understanding and empathy that a parent has for children and urge your people to play the role of parent or grandparent to the younger generation that they are seeking to reach. Being an actual parent is not required; instead, men and women just need to have a godly concern for the next generation. The older generation serving the younger generation is a powerful motif for creating the sense of urgency needed to jump-start a church toward revitalization. Pastor Gordon MacDonald's book *Who Stole My Church?* tells the story of one church finding renewal by making room for the next generation.

CREATING A GUIDING COALITION

Helping a church discover a sense of urgency is the first step in Kotter's process of leading change. The second step is to create a "guiding coalition." The role of this coalition is to state the vision for the changes needed to move the organization back to health and new life. Many young pastors, entrepreneurial by nature, take on the role of formulating the vision themselves and then try to convince the congregation to adopt it. In situations like this, clever vision statements are drafted, then recited (mostly by the pastor), and then soon forgotten. One of the biggest mistakes a pastor can make is to fly solo in this area of vision. While it is true that God speaks TO the individual pastor, it is also true that He speaks THROUGH the people and the circumstances. Each unique church setting will shape the vision God gives. No one person is smart enough to alone discern what God wants to do. The pastor must actively lead this process but must not get too far ahead of the flock.

The guiding coalition is the modern-day equivalent of biblical elders. Elders are the original form of church government, as old as tribal culture. In ancient cultures, the oldest members were regarded and admired as the wisest, simply by having lived longer and experienced more. It was also assumed that a group of such elders was wiser than any single individual. Churches, especially small churches, are tribal in nature and so characterized by a de facto eldership. It is this de facto eldership that ought to function as the guiding coalition.

It is de facto in that the members of this eldership may or may not comprise an official elder board. They may not even be committee chairs or hold any official positions in the church. But every church has an eldership function, certain individuals who by virtue of their personality, longevity, wisdom, faithfulness, and love have earned the right to lead in the church. When they speak, the congregation listens. These "elders" have a wisdom that is observed and respected by the body of church members. Granted, you may be required to form a guiding coalition out of the board of deacons or the church council. If that is not the case, seek to recruit the true "tribal elders" to make up the coalition. It may take some time to discern whom God's spirit is resting upon and whom He is choosing to lead, but it is worth the wait. Unless you have the support of these individuals, the vision you are proposing will probably fail.

I recall that I first observed this de facto eldership function in the early days of my pastorate. I was a "wet behind the ears" 30-year-old in the early years of my ministry. At that time, our church had a divided government of deacons and trustees. The deacons oversaw and maintained the spiritual life of the church, and the trustees managed the financial life. The deacons were fairly supportive of my ministry right from the start, but the trustees were somewhat suspicious. Whenever the deacons made a proposal for a ministry or program, if it was going to cost anything, they had to get the permission of the trustees. And often the trustees refused, simply saying "it wasn't in the budget." I spent a lot of time running back and forth between the two boards! I became increasingly frustrated at the inaction of the trustees, and that frustration sometimes boiled over into outbursts of anger on my part—something I was and am not proud of. I shared my anger with a pastor friend who often prayed for me. When he asked what my problem with the trustees was, I confessed that I did not trust them, that they controlled the funds and were holding back the church. He reminded me that the "gates of hell" are not able to hold back the church, and neither were my church's trustees. He told me my problem was that I did not trust God. I knew he was right. He suggested that I go to the trustees and, in true humility, apologize for my anger and tell them they would probably work better without me present. So, unless they needed me at a meeting, I would no longer attend. I honestly did not know what to expect, especially since the work of the deacons now would have no representative on the trustees. But I sensed that the Lord had really spoken through my friend and that something had to change; I could not carry on being angry. I went to the trustees, hat in hand, and apologized. I told them that I trusted them to act in the best interests of the church. They accepted my apology and said they would let me know if and when then needed me.

One of the trustees at the time was a retired business executive who had held a high post in a major American corporation. I noticed that he was always the last one to speak on issues, and when he did, everyone listened . . . and usually followed his advice. He was wise, had a good heart, and was a calming influence on the trustees and on me. Just as important, he had a genuine desire to see the church flourish. He had seen my frustration and anger and was sympathetic, noting that the church had long worked this way with the "deacons proposing and the trustees disposing." Recognizing that not much ever got accomplished, he agreed that we had to find a better way. A few weeks later, he invited me to lunch at his beautiful home and proposed what he called the "coordinating group." In industry, he said, when there were bureaucratic bottlenecks, a coordinating group would be formed to enhance communication, cut through red tape, and overcome obstacles hindering company goals. Why wouldn't the same strategy work at our church? He suggested a coordinating group consisting of the chair of the deacons, the chair of the trustees (the post he held), the treasurer, and me. We would meet once a month for about 45 minutes before work over breakfast to coordinate the work of the church, hence the name. Every person in the group was a respected church leader. I asked him if this was a legal committee according to the bylaws, and he replied that since it was an ad hoc committee, it was permitted in the bylaws. We would call it a "group" not a committee. It would not replace the work of the deacons or trustees, but it would coordinate that work so that we could begin to move the church forward. It made sense to me, and we began meeting. This was the answer God gave when my friend persuaded me to trust God and surrender the trustees to Him.

The coordinating group worked like a charm. We began to make plans together, not bouncing back and forth. If the treasurer said the church had the money, the chairs took the plans back to their respective committees, where they were usually accepted. With these well-respected and trusted leaders working hand in hand, we began to move the church forward. The system stayed in place for nearly 10 years, laying the foundation for an eventual shift from a committee-based governing system to an eldership, under the overall authority of the congregation, as it was a Congregational church. (In a later chapter, I spell out in more detail how this elder structure worked and why I believe it would work in most small-to-medium-size churches.)

What I realized was that the coordinating group was a "proto-elder" board in operation. In the tribal culture of our local church, it was a natural, organic form of leadership. It worked because all of the members were trusted, loved, proven leaders of the church. They had faithfully served the church in its years of conflict and decline; they had not quit, but had sought the good of the church. Even if many in the congregation still did not trust me, the newcomer, they trusted them. The authority of an eldership is founded on trust, whereas the authority of a committee system is frequently based on mistrust and on the protection of the various committees' constituencies. This is why it is so difficult to lead a church with a committee structure of governance.

I believe that most churches have men and women who are elders, even if not officially so. If you can prayerfully discern who those "elders" in your church are, you can begin to pray for them, encourage them, disciple them, and share your vision with them. In time, you can gather them and begin to share your heart for the vision of the church and hear what God is saying to them. If you have discerned and chosen well, the coalition will have the support of the congregation. Because you have mutually laid a foundation during the engagement and honeymoon seasons, the church knows that you are not going to abandon them and they have begun to trust you. To this partnership of you and this proto-eldership, God can begin to unveil His dreams for the church.

73

One final word about the so-called guiding coalition: Trust God that he has assembled the team that He wants. It may not be your dream team, but it is the one God is choosing to use. A slogan of legendary NFL coach Vince Lombardi has encouraged me countless times over the years: "WIN with the team you've got." Notice he didn't say, "PLAY with the team you've got"; every coach has to do that. He says find a way to *win* with *whatever* team you have been given because you will never have the perfect team. If Coach Lombardi's advice is not enough, hear the Apostle Paul's realistic assessment of his congregation in Corinth: "Not many of you were wise by human standards; not many were influential; not many were of noble birth. But God chose the foolish things of the world to shame the wise . . ." (I Corinthians 1:26b-27a).

DEVELOPING A VISION AND A STRATEGY

As we observed earlier, you cannot develop a vision with a committee. God speaks to individuals, who then speak to the people. However, God does not seem to give the entire vision to the pastor alone. He uses others to shape and guide the development of that vision, and those others are the "elders," or the guiding coalition.

A church's vision is different from its mission, but the two are related. A church's mission, often articulated in a mission statement, is its purpose statement. It is the reason the organization exists. It is a universal statement. Every church should have more or less the same purpose or mission statement because the Bible states it for us in the Great Commission (Matthew 28:18-20): "All authority in heaven and on earth has been given to me. Therefore, go and make disciples of all nations, baptizing them in the name of the Father, and of the Son, and of the Holy Spirit, and teaching them to obey everything I have commanded you. And surely I am with you always, to the very end of the age." The mission is also captured in the words of the Great Commandment (Matthew 22:37-40): "Love the Lord your God with all your heart and with all your soul and with all your mind. This is the first and the greatest commandment. And the second is like it: 'Love your neighbor as yourself.'" Furthermore, Acts 2 lists many of the functions of the first church. We can extract five or so specific purposes for the church, any church, from these verses. They can be worded many different ways, but essentially the big five are worship, fellowship, evangelism, discipleship, and service. Every vital church should state or at least imply these five purposes in a mission statement. The implementation of those purposes is specifically lived out in the vision of each church.

A vision statement, therefore, is *not* universal but different for every church. It is specific to the time, place, and circumstances of the local congregation. It is a future-oriented picture of what God is calling that particular church to be as it lives out the Great Commission and the Great Commandment in its community. It exists in the mind of Christ, and it is formed in the prayers and experiences of the pastor and the leaders. Chances are that, as a replant pastor, you already have the vision in your mind. It is there as you think and dream and pray about your church. If it is from God, then you will see it —envision it—as you seek God's will above all else. God is faithful and will gradually reveal it. In my experience, the vision is rarely revealed full-blown. Think about Moses. The vision was a people set free from bondage and led by God to their own homeland, but it was unfolded very gradually during a circuitous journey of 40 years, much of it lived in obscurity and humility.

In addition to being gradually revealed, a true divine vision is realistic, not grandiose. It is highly unlikely that God is calling anyone to build the Crystal Cathedral in rural Vermont or Willow Creek in northern Maine. A realistic, feasible vision is expressed in specific plans and actions through prayer and dialogue with the elders of the church. A wise pastor will work with his or her elders

75

to discern how the vision is to be crafted as specific plans and how those plans are to be implemented.

Often it is helpful to find a trusted outside guide to lead an elder team in the discerning of the vision. About 10 years before the close of my ministry, our church had outgrown our building. We had gone to two services about 15 years earlier, and to three services about 5 years earlier, and most recently, we had added a fourth service via video in an overflow area. We had expanded the building to its limits with a costly building campaign, but even that enlarged facility was now at capacity.

The staff and key volunteers were exhausted, and preaching three times each week and pastoring three congregations was wearing me thin. I knew we had to do something else. We were not deliberately trying to grow the church; we had assembled a faithful staff and elder board, and we were seeing people coming to Christ and being discipled. We were simply trying to be a healthy, balanced church. And God was drawing people to Christ through that health. To paraphrase Pastor Rick Warren, the goal of the church is not growth but health. And so a church should aim toward being spiritually healthy and let God give the growth. As pastors, we cannot grow churches any more than we can grow our children. Every organic entity grows itself, with the right balance of nutrition and other essentials. At that point in the life of our church, we were seeing tremendous growth and doing everything we could to faithfully receive and disciple the people that Christ was drawing to Himself. But we were simply running out of space and energy. Something had to be done.

We tried to purchase a vacant lot adjacent to the church that would enable us to expand the building. It was the only available space as the church was landlocked on every other side by its downtown location. The lot was valued at $300,000. The church made several generous offers, each of which was refused. Eventually, we offered $1 million, an enormous sum for our church. That offer was refused as well, and the owner named his price: $2.5 million. Clearly, he did not want to sell. I recall the day we received the news of his impossible counteroffer. It came on the day of a major snowstorm that paralyzed much of New England. The church offices were closed by the storm and I was at home, quietly trying to pray but feeling very discouraged as I reflected on this door for expansion being closed in our face.

I distinctly remember saying to the Lord, "Why are you letting this man block our plans?" Almost instantly I sensed God replying, "What makes you think HE is blocking your plans?" And in a moment I sensed that this was God calling us in a different direction. Immediately, I began dreaming of relocating the church. I imagined us selling our beautiful, historic downtown building, buying acreage in an outlying part of town, and building a much bigger building that would solve all of our space problems. I felt God had deliberately closed the door on the adjacent property because he had a much bigger plan in mind. You can bet I was excited. At our next elders meeting, I enthusiastically shared my vision but was crestfallen when no one else seemed to be excited. They could not imagine us leaving our strategic downtown location on which we had just spent millions to expand and upgrade. Now, I was thoroughly confused. Over the next few months at our elder meetings, we prayed and discussed every option we could think of to provide more space to accommodate the people God was bringing. It became more and more confusing.

Finally, someone suggested we bring in reinforcements: hire an outside professional to help us discern God's vision for the ministry. We contracted Steve Macchia, President of Leadership Transformations, Inc. He agreed to lead us in a church-wide discernment process. We would temporarily expand the elder board to include some former elders. This body would take the lead functioning as a guiding coalition but under Steve's direction. We would spend up to a year listening to God through his Word and through small group gatherings for prayer and discussion. We would provide material for individual prayer and hold large gatherings that Steve would help lead. We would conduct surveys of the congregation, as well as of individuals in the community who attended another church or no church. I preached sermons on prayer, discernment, our church's history, and the nature and purpose of the church. We put all options on the table, and through it all, we prayed. We called it our Year of Discernment.

Over the course of about eight months, we settled on four options. Steve Macchia even came up with alliteration to remember them.

- BUILD: Purchase land on the edge of town and build a new facility (this was my desire)
- BUY: Acquire the parcel of land adjacent to the existing church for the asking price of $2.5 million, although this was never popular with the church as they felt it amounted to extortion
- BIRTH: Plant a daughter church in a nearby community and send out a group to populate it
- BRANCH: Start a second site of our church in an adjacent town where about 30 percent of the congregation lived

We were lead in this discernment process by the Holy Spirit using the gifting of Steve Macchia. One of the most important exercises that Steve led was to have every parishioner write his or her choice of the four options on an index card. Then we all surrendered our preference to God by burning the cards in a fire, signaling the end of our individual desires and the beginning of seeking God's desire. The conclusion to the whole season of discernment came in a dramatic way. The elders gathered all of the input from the long process and spent a week in individual prayer. Eleven elders and I then met together and, in a secret ballot, voted for our choice among the four B's. When the ballots were read, the decision was unanimous. We had all chosen the Branch option of starting a second site. This decision was too big for the elders to own alone, so we convened a special meeting of the congregation. The elders' choice was explained and then approved by about 90 percent of the church. Those who disagreed expressed their reasons, but in the end, no one left the church over the decision. A year later, we launched a second site of the church in a town about 5 miles away. Now 8 years later, that second site is healthy in spite of several changes in pastoral leadership and location. Thanks to their confidence that God led the whole process, the young congregation there has been able handle these changes. The church had correctly discovered the will of God.

This is an example of a pastor and a group of elders reaching the point in their vision-seeking that they realized the need for more minds and listening hearts to discern God's plan for a church. This is one way in which guiding coalition helps a pastor to lead change.

COMMUNICATING THE CHANGE VISION

It is disheartening to realize how often the vision is "lost in translation." That is, a church labors prayerfully for months to discern the vision that Christ is revealing to his body, but then the leadership fails to communicate that vision consistently and effectively to the wider church.

Here are some communication mistakes that church leaders make. Do your best to avoid them.

1. Consolidating communication in one person, usually the pastor. If the pastor decides to be principal communicator, it will appear to be his or her vision alone. The elders, or the guiding coalition, need to co-communicate the vision and take full responsibility for it.
2. Failing to go through the proper communication channels. Key people hear about plans last and therefore do not fully support it.
3. Relying too much on mailings, bulletin announcements, website postings, and not enough on small, face-to-face

gatherings with various groups in the church, where the vision can be explained and concerns addressed.

4. Announcing that the vision will be implemented on a "trial" basis in case it does not work. This pretty much guarantees failure as the opposition simply waits it out or works to sabotage it.

5. Not fully trusting that this is Christ's vision for his church, opening a foothold for later doubt. If the leadership has prayerfully sought the Lord's leading, they need to trust that He has in fact led.

6. Not fully trusting that God will honor and bless the divinely ordained authority of the elders and the pastor (Romans 13) and therefore not boldly owning it.

7. Not realizing the need for redundancy in communication. In short, communicate, communicate, and communicate. Or, in military jargon, Tell them what you're going to tell them; tell them; and then tell them what you've told them.

8. Not adequately answering every question and objection to the vision.

9. Not giving a vision enough time to settle into the minds of the people. All change takes time to accept.

10. Not communicating enough with personal stories. It is the stories that humanize the vision.

11. Not getting broad-based "buy in" for the vision before it is implemented.

12. Not being able to articulate the vision succinctly. Kotter gives this useful rule of thumb: "If you cannot describe your vision to someone in five minutes and get their interest, you may have more work to do in this transformation process" (p. 81).

13. Using "clever" slogans. Pastors often try to put the vision into an original, creative slogan, but unfortunately most are neither original nor creative.

14. Not using the "bully pulpit" that the pulpit really is. Incorporate the vision into your preaching in a way that is natural and true to the text.

15. Not being bold enough in the vision. If the vision is from God, it will be bold and it will make sense to most people, both those inside the church and those outside. Nineteenth-century architect Daniel Burnham, who helped rebuild Chicago after the Great Fire, declared, "Make no little plans; they have no magic to stir men's blood and will probably themselves not be realized. Make big plans; aim high in hope and work." Church leaders and pastors should pay heed.

IMPLEMENTING THE VISION

The vision must move from ideas on paper and in the minds of the leaders to actual plans and ministries carried out in the life of the church. This "carrying out" activity involves the replant pastor catalyzing something new in the church. Remember your dual role as a "patient catalyst." If you have been patient during the honeymoon season and have earned the respect of the congregation and won the right to lead, now comes the season to change focus and initiate a work that will win new people to Christ. By now, you have accrued credits to lead the congregation in the work of evangelism and discipleship. Now, you are beginning the shift to reaching the new congregation that God is calling into being.

The following guidelines may help you stay on track as you start to give your plans flesh and blood.

1. As pastor, be prepared to give strong leadership. But challenge your committee people to help lead the new efforts. They may find it exciting to be engaged in life-changing ministry rather than routine committee work.

William McConnell in his book on church revitalization, *Renew Your Congregation*, tells the story of a contentious board meeting in his church over the color of paint for the church kitchen. It dawned on him that the reason the board members cared so much about the paint color was because that was the scope of their ministry involvement. When he was able to involve them in the more stimulating aspects of pastoral ministry, they cared less and less about trivial matters like paint color.

Likewise, seek the support, assistance, and leadership of your "tribal elders." And when new ministry leaders are called for, teach and apply the "spiritual gift" theology as the basis for recruiting and commissioning them. I'll describe this gift theology more in Chapter 13.

Always champion your leaders and celebrate their efforts and successes, not your own.

2. Consider "borrowing" leaders from other churches to show your congregation what is possible. These brothers and sisters may also be able train your leaders to develop your own ministry. This is part of Overseed's Hub Church strategy, in which stronger churches loan leaders to smaller churches in their geographical area to help launch new ministries.

3. Free up the church schedule so there is time and energy for you and your leaders. In a committee-based church, maintenance alone will consume all of the resources, so clear some space in the routine of the church.

4. Adequately fund any new initiatives; do not let them wither for lack of financial support. If the initiatives are not budgeted, seek "angel funding" from supportive individuals in the congregation.

5. Introduce the vision incrementally and gradually. Start only one or two new initiatives early on, and stay with them until they are established. Allow people to adjust to

change. Don't give up on a ministry too soon. It often takes several years before a ministry can become established and produce the results you have prayed for. Trust the vision that God showed you.

6. Stay away from big one-time events. Instead, introduce ongoing ministries that over time will reap lasting benefits. Everyone loves events because they grab a lot of attention, but the return on investment is typically small.

7. Do not try to reinvent the wheel. Originality is hard, and it can take years of trial and error to get a program right. Besides, there are many effective, tried and true ministries available. Many churches use proven outreach and discipleship ministries like Alpha, Divorce Care, MOPS, Pioneer Girls and Boys Brigade, Grief Share, Celebrate Recovery, Stephen Ministry, and others with great success. These ministries produce solid results for the Kingdom of God because they address real needs. Also, they have built-in training for leaders. I call them "cookbook" ministries because they have a winning recipe. A word of caution: follow the cookbook. If you meddle with the recipe or modify the program too much, the outcome will disappoint.

8. Always strive for excellence in implementing the vision. This does not mean perfection, just the best you can possibly do given the team you have. Alpha leadership training calls this the 100% Rule—give every task a 100% effort. A poor start to a ministry is worse than no start. It will just invite criticism. Excellence honors God and inspires confidence among the people.

9. Avoid any surprises. Alert the congregation in advance of what is coming. I realize that this may give those who oppose the new initiatives the opportunity to marshal resistance, but the opposite—blindsiding people—is worse.

10. Seek the level of approval you need. If the vision has already been approved, then move forward with the implementation. If you make a mistake, remember: it is often easier to ask for forgiveness than to ask for permission.

11. Do not push anything that you are not prepared to push forever. If God has not raised up the leaders to implement the vision, then trust that this is His way of slowing the process. Wait. Resist the temptation to jump in and lead something unless it is mission critical and you are prepared to lead it indefinitely.

12. Do things that also appeal to the congregation's self-interest so they can see the WIFM ("What's in it for me?") factor. Remember, the WIFM principle applies to almost every action in life. For us mere mortals, there is no such thing as a truly altruistic act. Only Jesus himself acted in a truly selfless way. The rest of us do things because we hope there is a benefit for us or ours. New initiatives must in some way appeal to the self-interest of the congregation. For example, in an older demographic, offer a Vacation Bible School for their grandchildren, not just for unchurched local families.

13. Create some small wins involving improvements to the church building and property itself. These tangible, visible updates are symbolic of the invisible revitalization that is happening spiritually. Often in spiritually declined churches, the church property has also been neglected. Some low-cost, sprucing up of the church grounds and building using church volunteers will signal a start to the spiritual renewal. It will also declare to the surrounding community that the church is still open for business.

14. Leverage events and activities that are familiar, such as turning a church supper from a fundraiser to a meal designed to foster community in the congregation. Instead

of eliminating a craft fair, transform it into a benefit for some local community project. I know of one local church that repurposed its supper fundraisers into a project that purchased protective vests for its local police department. In doing so, it won the praise of the whole city.

15. Do not leave your church until the vision has been engrained in the culture and until your leaders have embraced it. Too many pastors leave too soon, and churches that had begun to be revitalized slip either backward into their old ways or are taken backward by those who were never on board. As Kotter says, "Change sticks only when it becomes 'the way we do things around here,' when it seeps into the very bloodstream of the . . . body" (p. 14).

8

Minimizing and Managing Conflict

No one likes conflict. Unfortunately, though, conflict goes hand in hand with change, and change is necessary if a declining church is to be revitalized. Because pastors have to lead the change process, they are inevitably the focus of the conflict.

As we have already observed, conflict comes because change upsets the homeostasis that all living organisms, by their nature, work to achieve and maintain. In a dying or declining church, the same principle holds true. Congregations will go to great lengths to carry on as always and avoid even minor change.

Conflict in the church does have a unique feature, though. In any secular organization, change will be resisted simply because it upsets the equilibrium. In the church, however, there may also be a spiritual dimension to the conflict, which we'll address below in our discussion of managing conflict. But first, take heart! There are some change strategies that can help reduce the amount and intensity of conflict over change.

MINIMIZING CONFLICT

Go slow. The most effective way to minimize conflict is one we have already touched on: Introduce change gradually, incrementally. As common sense as this is, I am surprised by how often pastors try to make changes too quickly, the "ripping the bandage off" mindset mentioned earlier. It may work with bandages, but it seldom works with ministry.

Allow your leaders to help. Don't move forward with significant change without their support. If you have patiently earned their trust during the honeymoon season, then now you can draw on that trust and enlist their leadership help.

Follow your constitution. Put yourself under the governing authority in the church, whether that is a board of deacons, church council, elders, or the congregation. Romans 13:1 reminds us that we are all under authority and that God honors authority since he has ordained it. Even if we are not sure if those in authority over us are committed to Christ, we are still called to respect their authority. Remember that the Apostle wrote these words when evil Nero was likely the Emperor. We need the Holy Spirit as our ally in this season of leading change, so honor God by honoring the authority structure.

Explain the changes, again. Minimize conflict by continually communicating the reasons for the changes. Connect them back to the earlier work of the sense of urgency and the long-term vision. When possible, leverage your church's history to demonstrate precedence for the changes proposed.

Create stability zones. The phrase "stability zone" is ascribed to Alvin Toffler, American writer and futurist whose 1970 book *Future Shock* was a worldwide bestseller a generation ago (Schaller, 1993, pp. 44, 105). Stability zones are characterized by familiarity, enduring relationships, predictability, and continuity. They make it easier for congregations to handle and absorb change. A stability zone could be the decision to continue using the choir while the worship becomes more contemporary, or using familiar hymns in the praise set, or keeping a traditional service in place while adding a contemporary one. A pastor leading change must not see these stability zones as opposition or setbacks but as ways to help people adapt to change.

Resist killing "sacred cows." By sacred cow, I mean a custom or institution in the church that is supposedly beyond criticism or off-limits for any degree of tampering. If the tradition is not causing any great harm, keep your hands off, and let it die from benign neglect. I learned this lesson the hard way. Early on in my ministry I decided to make the worship service more efficient by eliminating having the ushers return to the front of the church after taking the offering. My idea was ostensibly to free up a little more time for prayer or music or preaching. I switched the dedication prayer to just before the offering. This way, the ushers would not have to make the second trip back to the front carrying the collection. This minor change also meant they did not have to transfer the offering from four plates to the customary red velvet bag, which was then placed in a single large silver platter for presentation. Nor did we need to sing the Doxology each week. I estimated that the change saved 1 or 2 minutes. I explained this to my deacons, implying that my motive, more time for "real" worship, was pure. In reality, my motives were mixed. I did want more time, but I also hated the look at that large, red velvet bag filled with all of the cash and offering envelopes. Especially at Easter or Christmas when stuffed with increased giving, it looked like big red basketball. Shortly after I made the arbitrary change, so many annoyed or angry people complained about missing the Red Bag that I was forced to retreat and reinstate the ritual. A wiser approach would have been to leave it alone until there were grumblings that the service was too long, at which time I could have asked the leaders what we might eliminate. Indeed, a few years later that happened and the Red Bag was history.

Be careful when dealing with bullies. Most declined churches have one or two bullies. These folks are often well intentioned, but their goal is to keep things the way they are, and their interaction is aggressive, either directly or in a passive aggressive way. They are sometimes shouters who angrily confront other people, especially in meetings. They have a critical spirit and hold everyone else to higher standard than themselves. In larger, healthy churches they can be disciplined and even given the spiritual care they desperately need. In small, declining churches, bullies have an oversized influence. They become what one pastor called "skunks." In the same way that a skunk will chase everyone away from a picnic, so church "skunks" drive away the kind, good-hearted people. Often in such a church, the fighting at meetings has been so fierce and unpleasant that the healthy people have left and only the "skunks" remain. In the resulting power vacuum, these well-intentioned but dysfunctional, unhealthy, unhappy people are able to wield power that they are not qualified to exercise. People who know them steer a wide path around them, and leadership tries to accommodate them. A new pastor and new people are not as wise. Thinking they are dealing with normal people, they are often drawn into their neurotic web and entrapped. I believe the Apostle Paul had "skunks" in mind in a very instructive passage in II Timothy:

> But mark this: There will be terrible times in the last days. 2 People will be lovers of themselves, lovers of money, boastful, proud, abusive, disobedient to their parents, ungrateful, unholy, 3 without love, unforgiving, slanderous, without self-control, brutal, not lovers of the good, 4 treacherous, rash, conceited, lovers of pleasure rather than lovers of God— 5 having a form of godliness but denying its power. <u>Have nothing to do with such people.</u> (II Timothy 3:1-5; underscore mine)

As nice Christians, we are surprised by the Apostle's stern exhortation to "have nothing to do with such people." We anticipate that he will tell us to treat these people nicely, or to try to help them or win them over. But he does not because the word of God is totally realistic. Paul, in effect, says that this kind of person wants you to engage with them so they can win what they see as a power struggle with their aggressive tactics. If Paul, who sometimes used salty language, were writing today, he might have appreciated George Bernard Shaw's advice: Never mud-wrestle with a pig; you'll both get dirty, but the pig will enjoy it.

I recently had to put Paul's counsel into practice. In my last pastorate, which was a small, declining church, there was one especially difficult bully. As a recent former treasurer of the church, he had managed to drive away many leaders, frequently accusing them of stealing or foolishly spending the church's money. Shortly after I arrived, he was removed from his post by the moderator and the church council. They had finally had enough of his insults and suspicions. He stopped attending church, but he would leave me angry phone messages demanding that I call him immediately to answer questions about church funds. My response was to wait at least a week before calling. (While I always advise pastors to return calls, you don't have to return every call immediately.) By the time I got back to him, he had usually calmed down, and I would still only divulge what he and every parishioner was entitled to know. I refused to be intimidated by him, and I refused to take the bait and get drawn into his trap.

Be careful to keep your own counsel in conflict situations. You must assume that every email, text, voice-mail message, letter, or conversation that you think is private will be passed on to others. Reread your emails or texts before you send them to be sure they are factual, gentle, and edifying. Always conduct yourself in a circumspect manner. Share information only with those whom you absolutely trust to keep confidences or on a need to know basis.

This includes your spouse. I strongly believe pastors should not share confidences with their spouse. Other professionals such as therapists or doctors do not go home and tell their spouses about their patients, and in my opinion neither should pastors. Does your wife or husband really need to know the sordid details of a tense board meeting or the personal problems of a parishioner? All pastors *do* need confidantes with whom they can share the burdens of ministry, but they should not be married to them. It is an unfair burden to put on spouses because they are powerless to affect or alleviate the situations but will still carry the anxiety. Also, a spouse who knows about a conflict but is unable to affect it may become resentful toward those involved. (It is especially important to shield your children from church conflict if you do not want them growing up hating the church.) Because conflict is a dynamic moving target, changing all the time, keeping your spouse current will consume a lot of time that is better spent praying together and maintaining a healthy relationship. A better approach is to seek out a mentor or wise colleague who can listen, pray, and coach you through it.

Congregants have a right to privacy and may test a pastor's trust by saying to the pastor's spouse something like: "I'm sure your husband has told you about my situation." A spouse needs to be able to honestly say, "My husband never betrays confidences, so I have no idea what you are talking about." When we keep confidences, trust is maintained. Over the years of my ministry, my wife was tested many times. She would honestly reply, with a little humor and false annoyance, "Jack never talks to me about anything!" I am proud of the fact that after 35 years my congregants were still sharing confidences with me. Nor did my wife have to bear the burdens of unpleasant board meetings or the pain that my parishioners were experiencing.

Insist on fair fighting rules. Ask your leadership board to agree to a few fairness rules. Top on the list would be refusing to accept anonymous criticism. If people do not have the courage to own up to their concerns or sign a complaint, then you should not entertain their censure. Also vigorously oppose any personal attacks, on yourself or others. You should not have to defend yourself or your family from ad hominem attacks. Discourage impromptu, non-scheduled meetings unless all parties are present. Limit online meetings because not everyone has continuous access to personal email. Ask your leaders not to dump complaints on you on Sunday mornings, especially just before the start of worship. Unless it is an emergency, it can wait until you are in the office. Don't triangulate relationships by conveying concerns to others through third parties, and don't allow others to do that to you. Insist on persons bringing their concerns face to face.

I know of some churches that form Pastoral Relations committees, which create a channel for anonymous criticism of the pastor. This is an unfair and unhealthy practice. If your church does not have such a committee, discourage its formation. If it does, insist that it require all critics to bring their concerns to you directly. This is biblical (Matthew 18:15-17).

Prepare well for meetings. Large, or open meetings, which are common in congregationally governed churches, can be very unpleasant and even destructive to church unity if they are allowed to get out of hand. Chaotic town-hall-style meetings, controlled by a few angry members, will drive the civil members away. A good way to prepare is to first hold a pre-meeting with all the leaders present. When the leadership is unified, a few "screamers" are unable to control the large meeting. It may also be important to hold hearings with the congregation before a major vote. This way, you show respect to and get input from the wider church body. Also holding a potluck meal with humorous skits before the meeting can strengthen the bond of fellowship and show that while we take the ministry seriously, we do not take ourselves seriously. A pre-meeting might also include a ceremony to honor various servants and leaders. Above all, prepare spiritually for the meeting, with the leaders yielding in prayer to the Head of the body. Especially pray for the fruit of the spirit, including self-control, to be manifested in the lives of the members, the leaders, and the pastor. Conflict can be an opportunity to engage people with the gospel and biblical thinking, though typically in private not during an open meeting.

Conflict can be minimized with these common sense "best practices." But if conflict does erupt openly, it is essential to manage it so that it doesn't burn out of control like a wildfire. Unmanaged conflict splits churches and ends pastorates.

MANAGING CONFLICT

Don't allow the conflict to get personal. This is easier said than done. The individuals resisting your leadership blame you for the conflict, and you may be blaming them. But it is Christ who has called you to shepherd this flock through the difficult work of recapturing the church's mission in the world. It is vital that you remember His call, and that He who calls you is faithful and will accomplish his purposes (I Thessalonians 5:24). Conflict is frequently part of the price of being obedient to that call. If we lose sight of our call, then we risk taking the conflict personally.

If you are being obedient to Christ in leading change, and if you are gently, slowly, patiently bringing your flock along, then chances are you are not the problem. Now, you may become the problem if you are too forceful and too set on having your own way. But if you have led slowly and lovingly, don't allow the enemy to accuse you. The greatest crisis in my own pastorate came during my tenth year in the church. One would think that, by then, the worst would be over. It happened this way:

A small but influential group of long-time members became increasingly alarmed as newer, younger, more Christ-centered members began to take positions of leadership. This group began to gather various complaints about me in what I call a "fishing expedition," an attempt to dredge up every possible criticism or grievance from any source, past or present, against a pastor, and to weave the strands into whole cloth. My opposition had decided it was time for me to go. They hoped to call for a congregational meeting to vote on whether I should stay or be removed as pastor. But they could only garner 20 of the 25 petition signatures needed

93

to call such a meeting, so they abandoned that strategy in favor of private meetings in their homes to recruit more support. What they didn't know was that one of their number was intensely loyal to the church and to me because we had helped her through a difficult divorce when her husband left her. This woman had given her life to Christ and now knew the group and their actions were wrong. She told the deacons and me everything they were planning. This was a very difficult time for me and my wife—without doubt the lowest point in my entire ministry. This group had managed to cast enough doubt about me and my ministry that even some of my closest friends began to believe that I was the problem. It had gotten so bad that I was actually thinking of resigning rather than continue in the face of such opposition. But because I was called to this ministry, the God who called me was also carrying out his purposes in this trial. He spoke to me powerfully through two people in that season of conflict.

The first person was my own dear father. Though not an educated man, he was a lifelong student of the Bible. One spring night he and I were driving to our camp in Maine to go fishing the next day. I unburdened my heart to him. He shared from memory portions of the book of Nehemiah and reminded me that the Prophet's opponents were spreading a false report that Nehemiah was the problem. However, it was the Lord who had called Nehemiah to Jerusalem to rebuild the wall. My father reminded me that Nehemiah's opponents kept trying to arrange a meeting with him, ostensibly to discuss the problem, all the while wanting to remove him by killing him. Similarly, and not surprisingly, my opponents kept calling for some kind of public meeting to "discuss" the problem. They lacked any real issue to complain about; they simply did not like the fact that new people were coming into leadership and bringing changes with them. Heeding my father's counsel and citing Nehemiah, I asked my deacon board to resist the call for public meetings and instead give the complainants a chance to have their concerns heard by the deacons. In the end, four people came to that meeting, all from one family. The board heard their complaints and realized they were simply unhappy that the church was changing and they were losing influence. This family had wielded much authority in the past, having successfully forced the resignation of the two previous pastors. The board deliberated for a week and then issued their decision; finding no substance to their complaints, they urged them to cease their opposition and honor their membership vows. For the next two months these four individuals continued to sing in the church choir each week, but when I stepped into the pulpit to preach, they would stand up and walk out. They soon left the church altogether, along with two friends they had persuaded to join them. We lost six members. In spite of repeated attempts by our board and me to seek reconciliation, they never returned. God used that spring evening counsel by my beloved father to change the course of my ministry and that church.

The other person God used to speak into this same situation was the dynamic pastor of St. Paul's Episcopal Church in Darien, CT, Rev. Terry Fullham. As this discontent and conflict were brewing, I attended a pastors' conference at St. Paul's hosted and lead by Dr. Fullham. St. Paul's was at the center of church revitalization in the 1980s and 1990s (you may have heard of the "Miracle at Darien.") During the conference, Dr. Fullham met with me personally as I shared what was happening in my church. He prayed for me and then startled me by saying he believed that God Himself had brought about the conflict. He advised me to stop trying to avoid it and to let the board take the lead in confronting it. He reminded me that God had ordained the board's authority (Romans 13:1). He then added what he felt was a word directly from the Lord, namely that God was using me to "break the ungodly power chain" that this family had wielded over the church for decades. As soon as he said this, I knew in my spirit that God had spoken to me, and that I was neither to take the blame nor regret the conflict. That word set me free to lead the church forward. And after these individuals left, for the first time since I had begun my pastorate 10 years earlier, the church itself was also set free to fully follow Christ's lead.

Do not take the conflict personally, but instead trust that God is in the midst of it. This is necessary to be able to stay the course through to victory.

Discern when the conflict is ungodly and dark in nature. Signs that this might be the case are when criticism becomes personal and irrational, or when the pastor's family is the target. Or when the anger is expressed in hateful, anonymous letters. Or when the anger is far out of proportion to the supposed offense or involves other strong emotional behaviors, such as crying or screaming. Or when the conflict centers on the issue of biblical authority, or the centrality of Christ, or a ministry of healing or deliverance. Since the Evil One is known as "the accuser," do not be surprised when opposition comes in the form of accusations. Ephesians 6:12 reminds us that our conflict is not "against flesh and blood, but against the powers of this dark world and against spiritual forces of evil . . . ."

Do not demonize your opposition. When we are in the throes of a church battle, it is easy to feel that those opposing us are our enemies. In opposing our effort to lead the church in a more biblical direction, they are ultimately opponents of Christ, whose church it is. Since they are opponents of Christ, we must not resort to the tools of the Enemy such as gossip, or slander, or accusations.

However misguided, insecure, or controlling your opponents might be, they certainly believe they have the best interests of the church in mind. Often, they are previously loyal members who have contributed a great deal of time, effort, and resources to the church. Some time spent listening to their concerns (in one-on-one conversations, not public meetings) will often diffuse the issue. As I look back over my early days in the pastorate, I realize I should have done more listening, and some conflicts might have been avoided.

Know yourself. Be what Rabbi Edmund Friedman calls "self-differentiated," or in lay terms, know who you are, and be comfortable in your own skin. Spiritually speaking, we pastors should be secure in our identity in Christ and in His call on our lives. This is something that comes as we anchor our lives in prayer and God's Word. We thus learn to deflect the arrows of the enemy with the armor of God (Ephesians 6). Remember, as the pastor, you are the only person in the church who has been called to lead and affirmed by the whole congregation following a long and deliberate search process. Trust that God has called you to your post, according to His plan. Do not surrender that call.

Be part of a pastors group. Join or gather a pastors support group with whom you can share your burdens so they can encourage you from the Word, keep you in prayer, and hold you accountable. Ideally, the group would include some pastors in similar replant situations or a coach who has experienced church conflict and successfully led the church through it. In Overseed we call these support groups Replant Pastors Cohorts.

I recommend a group based on theological affinity, as well as similarity in terms of revitalization. Local clergy ministerial fellowships and denominational clergy groups have their value, but when a pastor is engaged in the conflict that comes with church revitalization, it is important to have the support of others who have faced, or are facing, the same thing.

Along the same lines, find a coach. Look for an older, wiser pastor with whom you can share your burdens. Choose someone who is both trustworthy and competent to help. Ask them to pray for you regularly. A good coach is a guide who has been over the trail before and knows where the pitfalls and obstacles are.

Call in an outsider. In extreme conflict, outside intervention by someone in authority may be necessary. Sometimes the situation evolves out of control to the point where the conflict threatens to split the church, and all attempts by the involved parties fail to resolve it. This is the role of a denominational executive—and a good reason to be denominationally affiliated.

Implement stronger, not weaker, membership requirements. As churches decline, it is tempting to lower membership standards to make it easier to gain members. A church needs to have a clear and reasonable process for both adding and removing members. Inactive members become political pawns for both sides in times of conflict when every vote is needed. However, inactive members usually vote in favor of the status quo and against a pastor seeking to revitalize a church. In political terms, this is called "voting the dead." Author and pastor Mike McKinley, in his delightful book *Church Planting Is for Wimps*, says that an up-to-date and accurate membership roster gives "legitimacy to the decisions of the congregation" (p. 60). Offer membership classes frequently, and when appropriate, be flexible in membership requirements depending on the applicants. For example, you will need to spend more time discipling a new believer before suggesting membership, but make joining easier for mature Christians who are transferring membership from another church. Whether we like it or not, churches are political organizations, and pastors need to be comfortable with the political aspect of church life when it is required to advance the mission. Remember, the Apostle Paul also played the political game when it was necessary, calling on his Roman citizenship to help advance the gospel.

Exhibit the fruit of the spirit in your life. As painful as they might be, seasons of conflict are tremendous growth opportunities for pastors and churches. The Apostle James challenges us to find joy in the trials we face because we know God is at work forming our faith and maturing the church. As pastors and leaders in our churches, God wants to produce in our lives the characteristics of genuine faith: "love, joy, peace, patience, kindness, goodness, faithfulness, gentleness, and self-control" (Galatians 5:22-23). Never are these qualities more needed than when we are in the midst of conflict. A sermon series on the fruit of the spirit would be very timely when a church is fighting, but only if the pastor is showing the way with his or her own life.

Seek healing and reconciliation between the "warring" factions whenever possible. Often this is not possible. The Bible is very realistic in assessing the likelihood of reconciliation when Paul says to the Romans, "If it is possible, as far as it depends on you, live at peace with everyone" (Romans 12:18). I know of a pastor who felt led by God to reach back several decades to try to heal church splits that had taken place under previous pastors. With his guidance, church leaders went to former members whom the church had wounded and, with tearful expressions of sorrow, asked for their forgiveness. Although none of those visited ever came back, the genuine gesture helped set the church free to move forward with new life in Christ. However, sometimes reconciliation is just not possible. One party might no longer be living or might have rebuffed every effort toward healing. In such cases, we must leave the situation in God's hands and move on.

REACHING A TIPPING POINT

In this third season of a revitalization pastorate, a time of change and conflict, you have been intentionally transitioning from patient chaplain to catalyzing change agent—deftly straddling the dual role but definitely changing focus. With grace, you are effectively minimizing and managing the inevitable conflict. Some members who have resisted your leadership have been won over; others have chosen to leave rather than oppose; a few have become inactive and may continue to try to undermine your leadership from a distance.

But by and large, with the aid and power of the Spirit, your revitalization ministry is unfolding and bearing fruit. Trust the process. This season will soon be replaced by the next. Look for the signs of the changing season.

There often comes a discernable tipping point at which the congregation embraces the pastor's leadership and a new season of fruitfulness takes hold. In my experience, this tipping point typically occurs 7 to 10 years into a renewal pastorate, depending on many variables, including the following.

The Starting Point

Every church begins the renewal process at a different starting point and so will have a different tipping point. It is crucial for a pastor to recognize this fact and spend time at the beginning of his or her ministry discerning where the church is with regard to renewal. For some churches, the renewal process was already begun by a predecessor and is well underway. For other churches, the decline was not addressed by previous pastors. Churches also vary greatly in the stages of decline they are in. Some churches have not been in decline for long, and the path to revitalization will be shorter. Other churches have declined to the point of near death, and renewal may not be possible at all. The tipping point may never be reached.

The Skills and Gifts of the Pastor

Since church revitalization is all about leadership, the impact of the skills and spiritual gifts of the pastor cannot be overstated. The interpersonal skills of a pastor can have an enormous effect on the process and bring about a tipping point sooner. I believe it helps if the pastor is effective in reading social cues and forming relationships.

As in any arena of leadership, the personal qualities of the pastor count for a lot. In their book *Resilient Ministry,* authors Burns, Chapman, and Guthrie use the phrase "Emotional Intelligence"

(EQ) to describe the ability to manage your emotions and respond appropriately to the emotions of others. EQ involves a person's "self-awareness, self-management, social awareness, and relationship management" (p. 103). The authors further define EQ as "the ability to proactively manage your own emotions (EQ-self) and to appropriately respond to the emotions of others (EQ-others) . . . Without the ability to understand our own emotions—as well as our strengths, limitations, values, and motives—we will be poor at managing them and less able to understand the emotions of others" (p. 103). The authors cite evidence that our emotional intelligence can continue to develop as we navigate relational experiences of life (p. 106). In the early days of my ministry, I allowed my anger and frustration to damage a number of relationships. This relational "carnage" was not good and not necessary, but God in his mercy taught me much in these difficult lessons. I grew as a result and learned to deal more gently and kindly with those with whom I disagreed. So be aware of your own EQ and look for evidence that you are becoming more emotionally intelligent. Recognize your feelings and express them appropriately. Be a good listener, and convey genuine concern and empathy for others. Be secure in your relationship with God so you are not easily victimized by the strong emotions of others.

Emotional intelligence also means being able to receive criticism without responding in anger or becoming discouraged or devastated. It enables you to evaluate criticism to determine if there legitimacy in it. It allows you to resolve and heal conflict rather than avoid it and/or hope it goes away. It also makes it possible for you to agree or disagree with others and, on your part at least, move beyond conflict. Pastors with increasing emotional intelligence will be better able to lead their churches through the conflict that accompanies change. Authors Pete Scazzero (*The Emotionally Healthy Church*) and Paul David Tripp (*Dangerous Calling*) have been especially helpful to me and to the pastors I coach in growing in emotional intelligence. The gifts and relationship skills a pastor brings to his or her ministry will have a high impact on leading a congregation to the tipping point.

The History and Size of the Church

A church's history influences the time it takes to reach the tipping point. What is the historical memory of the church? Was the church previously a large church? If so, the resistance to growth will probably be less. A church that has always been small may find it hard to envision anything different and may struggle to embrace new people coming into the fellowship. The church's image in the local community is also a factor in how renewal will take place. I know of one pastor, before accepting a call, asked the other clergy in the community how the church was viewed.

The present size of the church also matters. There are churches that are too small to be revitalized. Unless you bring people with you or are a gifted evangelist, you may not be able to muster the people resources to even begin the process. A church with sufficient members or adequate endowment funds to maintain the institution will at least provide a stable starting point.

Local Demographics

Local demographics can obviously play a huge role in the revitalization process and moving a church to the tipping point. Trying to renew a church in a tiny rural community, or in sparsely populated farm country, is probably going to be harder than in a community where there is a steady supply of people who have no prior experience with your church. Clearly, trying to revitalize an older, white congregation in a predominantly non-white community (without trying to reach that community) is also going to be a challenge. Since church revitalization is by its very nature a missionary effort, it is essential for a church to reach the people who surround it.

I realized this when I began my first pastorate. My church was a mostly older, blue-collar, high-school-educated congregation, many of Scottish descent, living within walking distance. We were located in a community with a large Roman Catholic population. The town was also an increasingly ethnically diverse, white-collar, college-educated community where growth was occurring in the outlying areas of the town. If the church was to live, we had to be a missionary to the people who were increasingly there. Now many years later, that church has a large formerly Roman Catholic and somewhat ethnically diverse, white-collar congregation. It helped that the church is located in a growing community at the intersection of two interstate highways and near a major metropolitan area.

It is not accidental that after Apostle Paul's first missionary journey to Cyprus and the small cities of eastern Asia Minor, he took his second and third journeys to the great cities of the ancient world like Athens, Corinth, and Ephesus, with a goal to go to Rome. The switch toward larger, more dynamic, metropolitan places was probably because church planting is easier than in small, isolated places. I am guessing the same is true for replanting. However, the sovereign God calls us where he wants us, and we trust him to give the increase regardless of the location.

When the tipping point comes, some members who have been resisting the pastor's leadership will decide to leave. Hopefully it is because they realize there is no place for insubordination in the body of Christ, and that if they cannot support the church leadership, they should worship elsewhere. Realistically though, they may leave because they have lost the power to will their way. If possible, part company as friends, but either way it is important to let them go. It is even more important to honor those members who decide to stay, especially if they are older, and have weathered the many changes that have taken place to bring the church back to health. These people are true saints who put the will of God ahead of their own comfort and preferences. When I retired from my church after 35 years, the congregation held a banquet in my honor. At one point I asked people to stand who had been members when I arrived, out of the several hundred people who were there, about 15 people stood—most had been retired or nearing retirement when we had arrived and so were now in their 90s. I called each by name and thanked them for their faithfulness to Christ and their loyalty to me. They had lovingly and faithfully navigated the turbulent waters of change and never gave up on me, or the church. Very appropriately, everyone stood in their honor and applauded their faithfulness.

9

The Primacy of Preaching

If you've ever read *Moby Dick*, you may recall that Ishmael attends a worship service at the little Whaleman's Chapel in New Bedford, MA, before setting out for Nantucket and his epic whaling voyage. Father Mapple is the clergyman. He preaches—on Jonah—from a very strange pulpit. It looks like the prow of a ship, which he reaches by climbing up a ship's ladder. Behind him is a painting of a ship in a storm observed by an angel looking down from the clouds.

Melville is invoking the ancient Christian symbol of the church as an ark of safety and rescue on the stormy seas of life. The pulpit is the prow, the foremost part of the ship that cuts through the water, representing the proclamation of God's word. God's word, as it is preached, taught, studied, read, believed, and followed, is the leading edge of God's powerful transforming effect on individuals, families, societies, nations . . . and churches. I cannot overstate the importance of biblical preaching in the revitalization process. That's why I'm devoting an entire chapter to this topic.

Worship is the most important function of the Church, and preaching is the "center of gravity" of worship (Martin, 1985, p. 66). More than anything else in your ministry, God will use your faithful, godly, biblical preaching to transform your congregation. In study after study on the reasons why people attend or join a church, preaching is cited as the number one reason. J. Kent Edwards mentions one such study in his book *Deep Preaching: Creating Sermons That Go Beyond the Superficial*. He reports on a 2005–2006 survey conducted by the Talbot School of Theology among 1,081 people of all ages who had joined an evangelical church within the previous two years. The top reason stated was the "Preaching of the Pastor" (p. 41).

My own 35-year ministry in the same church convinces me that this is true. I certainly would never win any awards for my preaching, but through the years members of my congregation told me that hearing the word of God each Sunday was the most important thing about our church. Most of the evangelism that took place in our church was the quiet evangelism of people hearing the gospel (the good news of Jesus Christ) on Sunday mornings and believing in Jesus Christ. On occasion, I gave invitations to receive Jesus Christ as Lord and Savior, and I believe it is important for a pastor to do that. However, I found that most of those who later declared a commitment to Christ had discovered Him by hearing the gospel preached. Of all the other functions of the local church, such as small groups, mission, community service, none is more vital than biblical preaching. The preaching of the word of God week after week (undergirded with prayer) is the single most effective tool to bring about church revitalization. Biblical preaching is the key evangelistic and discipleship ministry in the local church. As Tim Keller reminds us, if your preaching makes the people in the pews wish their neighbors were there to hear it, they will bring their neighbors. Because preaching is so important, and because effective biblical preaching is so difficult, it's not surprising that we face many challenges in our preaching ministry. Let me offer some thoughts about the task of preaching.

PREPARING YOUR SERMONS

Allow Adequate Preparation Time

You will never have enough time to be fully prepared to preach. Weekly sermon preparation has been compared to writing a song each week and then singing it unfinished on Sunday morning. I've never written a song, but I know I rarely ever felt completely ready when I stepped to the pulpit. We preachers have to rely on the Holy Spirit to fill in our deficiencies. Early on in my ministry, I left sermon preparation until late in the week. I must confess that many times, in that first year or two, I was working late Saturday night and getting up at 4am on a Sunday to finish. I recall the anxiety it caused me, the stress it put on my family, and the regret afterward of knowing I could have done better. It was that anxiety, stress, and regret that eventually led me to start preparing earlier in the week. I consistently needed 15–20 hours of preparation each week. I was fortunate to be in full-time ministry. Since most revitalization pastors today are bi-vocational, 10 hours is probably more realistic. Sunday morning worship is consistently the one hard and fast deadline a pastor faces each week. Many other aspects of pastoral ministry can be postponed, but the weekly sermon cannot. So start early, and schedule in the time you need to prepare.

Preach Sermon Series

Preaching sermon series helps with preparation. I found that preaching unrelated sermons week to week meant that much of my study time was spent just trying to think of what to preach. So I started planning sermon series either from a book of the Bible or based on a broad topic, such as the Holy Spirit, prayer, or sin and forgiveness. This approach helped with the preparation because I could be thinking ahead about upcoming messages. I would create a separate file for each message in the series, and then as I did exegetical study or as homiletical ideas came to me, I would drop them into the appropriate file. As any preacher knows we are always thinking about what we are preaching. I found that the Holy Spirit often brought to mind insights about a future text and ideas about how to illustrate it. The earlier I knew in advance what I was preaching, the better I felt about my preparation.

Take a Break

Many pastors find that after about two months of weekly preaching, they need to take a break in order to be working ahead. Fortunately, I often had a seminary student as an intern. I would conduct the rest of the service that week, but have my intern do the sermon. I could then also observe and coach him. On those weeks, I would steal away to a retreat place for a day to pray and work on the next series. I found that my anxiety in preaching ebbed and flowed in direct proportion to how far in advance I was preparing. Cultivate relationships with people—for example, retired pastors in your church or nearby; underemployed colleagues; staff members; elders in your church—who can provide occasional backup so that you can take a break when needed.

Develop Your Own Planning Process

It's important for you to develop and fine-tune your own planning process. Let me share mine with you, as an example. It is one that many pastors use, and it is one that works. Because I am more left-brained than right, I found the exegetical task of ferreting out the meaning of the text and preparing an outline much harder than the homiletical task of preparing the content of the message. Once I understood the text and could form an outline, my creative side went to work finding illustrations and applications. I was fortunate to be taught the "Big Idea" system of preaching in my time at both Fuller Theological School and Gordon-Conwell Theological

Seminary. This approach involves studying the biblical text to discover the one essential (Big) idea in a unit of Scripture. Then, from that key idea, pose a question and provide an answer. Every sermon needs to pose a question to the congregation and then, from the same Scripture, provide God's answer. This is the dialogical nature of preaching: we are asking and answering the Bible's questions. And because the Bible is asking and answering life's questions, we can be sure it addresses the needs and issues of our congregation.

By focusing on the big ideas of the Bible, you ensure that you are preaching the huge, universal truths of God, not the small, limited ideas of human culture. Though he was speaking about the secrets of the universe, not the Bible, Albert Einstein once declared, "I want to know God's thoughts, everything else is details." If you adopt the goal of the big idea approach, to discover God's thoughts, then usually the details of the message come more easily. Edwards' book *Deep Preaching* includes a clear and thorough explanation of the big idea method of sermon preparation. He emphasizes going into your "closet" to pray and earnestly ask God both to unlock the truths of His word to your understanding and to help inspire you to put flesh on those truths for your people.

Make sure your preaching is gospel preaching. Gospel preaching focuses on the central act of our salvation history: the coming of Jesus Christ, the Son of God, to live, suffer, die, be raised again, and ascend to the Father. Gospel preaching isn't limited to just preaching the four gospels, for ALL of Scripture contains the gospel. Jesus Christ and His redemptive acts are anticipated in the Old Testament and fulfilled and explained in the New. The unity and wholeness of the Bible has been stated this way: The New Testament is concealed in the Old, and the Old Testament is revealed in the New.

The content of your preaching will depend on where your church is in the revitalization process. If you are in the beginning stages of revitalizing a church without a long history of biblical preaching, your focus will be on the main gospel message and may center on the four gospels. On the other hand, if your church has a history of biblical preaching and commitment to Christ but is inwardly focused, your messages may deal with the doctrine and mission of the church and flow from the New Testament epistles.

As a new congregation is catalyzed within an existing congregation, a pastor must preach to both groups on Sunday mornings. As challenging as this is, each message must speak to those older, lifelong believers as well as the younger, brand-new believers and the curious seekers. It was probably no different for the early church, which was populated with devout Jewish converts who knew the Scriptures and with pagan God-seekers who had no scriptural point of reference. Thankfully, because we are preaching the word of God, we don't have to "make it relevant." It is universally relevant to every age and in every culture.

PREACHING YOUR SERMONS

Learn to Preach Extemporaneously

Extemporaneous preaching involves working from notes and not a manuscript. It requires extensive preparation but leaves the preacher freedom and flexibility in the precise wording of the sermon. Extemporaneous preaching follows the "talking points" style of public speaking that is very popular today, and very effective. It allows the speaker to be free from notes and to engage the audience with eye contact. It also enables the speaker to read the audience and to make tweaks to the message in progress depending on audience reaction and the Holy Spirit's prompting. Some pastors still read their sermons. In my opinion, this is deadly for the congregation; it is the fastest way to put them to sleep.

In order to speak extemporaneously, you *must* first write out a complete manuscript. It is in writing a manuscript that you make all your transitions smooth, all of your sentences complete, and all of your stories succinct. There were times in my preaching ministry when in order to save preparation time, I would go directly from my outline to my preaching notes. This was always a mistake. The written manuscript is an essential part of connecting all the dots of your thinking and preparation.

Then, convert the manuscript into one page of notes and file the manuscript away. You won't need it in the pulpit, but you now have a complete copy to distribute to the congregation later or for your own future use. So, this sermon preparation process has gone from your prayer and study time, to the big idea and an outline, to a manuscript, to a single page of notes. There is one final step.

The last step in extemporaneous preaching preparation is to say through your message. Relying on your notes, preach your sermon to yourself. You can actually speak your message out loud or simply "say" it in your mind. In my early days, I did this two or three times for each sermon, usually speaking aloud, sometimes from the pulpit, on a Saturday night. Later on, I found that saying it twice in my mind was sufficient. Do not skip this very important step in your preparation. Saying your sermon through allows you to become quite familiar with your message without actually memorizing it, thus freeing you from your notes. Each time you say it through, your brain forms a word path for conveying that idea. So by the time you preach, you have multiple ways that you can express each idea. This is not the same as memorizing the message. I strongly advise you not to try to memorize your sermons. In memorizing, your brain has only one word path, and if you forget that path, you are stuck. Also, the memorized version will be in the preacher's written language, which is different— more formal and stilted—than our colloquial spoken language. When you preach extemporaneously, your congregation will feel as if you are talking directly to them, because you are.

In an unexpected, unplanned way, I discovered that I could deliver a prepared message without notes. One Sunday morning in my early days of pastoring, I stepped into the pulpit and opened my Bible to where I thought I had placed my sermon notes. To my horror, they were not there. I then remembered that I had left them on my office desk. A sense of panic swept over me, and I instantly began to consider all my options. Then a sense of calm came over me, which must have been the Holy Spirit, and I realized that I knew the message well enough from saying it through to carry on without notes. I never forgot my notes again, but that lesson taught me that if I had done my preparation to the best of my ability, following the process I was taught, then God would give me freedom in the pulpit to remember my message, follow His promptings, and catch the congregation's cues. I strongly urge pastors to do the difficult, big-idea work, then write a manuscript, convert it to a page of notes, say it through, and trust both your process and the Holy Spirit.

Resist the Temptation to Plagiarize

Effective biblical preaching is hard work, and it takes time. Sometimes in order to avoid the hard work or to save precious time, we are tempted to plagiarize. Plagiarism is a serious problem and has cost many a newspaper columnist his or her job. Columnists, like preachers, are constantly working under a deadline. For both professions plagiarizing is a real temptation. Never before has so much good sermon material been available, and some denominations may even encourage their pastors to take advantage of it in order to ensure they are preaching biblically sound sermons. The Roman Catholic Church requires its thousands of parish priests to use the same officially prepared homily in all of its churches to guarantee that Catholic theology is universally taught and applied. Given all of the tasks that a pastor has to attend to each week, using someone else's sermon is very tempting. A pastor can easily justify the practice by saying the preparation time saved could be better spent in evangelism, discipleship, or caring for the flock. But this ignores the fact that the primary way God has called us to evangelize, disciple and care for our flock is with the preached word of God. A good reminder of this is Acts 6: the Apostles chose to spend their time preaching and praying rather than doing other much-needed parish work.

Something else happens when we plagiarize, something even more dangerous than dishonesty. WE don't show up. When we use someone else's message, THEY are in the pulpit, not us. The incredible thing about God is that He loves incarnational, relational ministry. He could have chosen to continue to send his word via the Prophets. But in His wisdom, in the fullness of time, He didn't send more Prophets but came himself. In order to convey the great wideness of his truth and love, he had to come and show us himself.

Your people don't want a perfectly crafted message (though they may think they do). They want you. I recall one of the first summers in my church when I lined up two outstanding Gordon-Conwell professors to fill my pulpit while I was on vacation. When I got back, I asked my deacons how the guest preachers were. One dear deacon said, "They were ok, but we really like your sermons, pastor." Both of these professors were godly, gifted, veteran preachers. There is no question they were better preachers than me, but their problem was, they weren't me. My church had called me to be their shepherd, with all of my flaws and inexperience.

When we plagiarize, we also rob the Holy Spirit of the opportunity to do his work in our lives that comes from wrestling with the text. What preacher hasn't come under the conviction of the Holy Spirit as he or she has studied a text and prepared to challenge a congregation to obey it?

Let's be honest, most of us have plagiarized sermons, at least parts of them. It's like telling white lies, or thinking lustful thoughts; we have all done it, but it's not right and we don't feel good about it. Like those columnists who get caught sooner or later, a plagiarizing pastor will get caught, either by an observer or by his own conscience. Recently I was worshipping in the church of a young, up-and-coming pastor. His message was good; in fact it was so good that I suspected it might not all be original. While I was chatting with him after the service, an older woman came up and told him how much she enjoyed his message. She then said with all sincerity, not at all accusingly, "I heard Andy Stanley give that same message this week; he told the same stories you did." My young friend was clearly embarrassed. I invited him to lunch that week and waited until he brought up the incident. He admitted he was under a lot of time pressure and had preached Stanley's message almost verbatim. I reassured him that we were all guilty but that there is a better way. If the same situation should occur in the future, he might use another pastor's outline but give that pastor credit and flesh it out with his own content. I once heard the great pulpiteer Harold J. Ockenga preach in chapel at Gordon-Conwell Seminary, of which he was the founder and president. He said right at the outset, "I want to give credit to Dr. Stephen Olford (Pastor of Calvary Baptist Church, New York City) for my outline this morning." He then went on to preach his own message using Olford's outline. I think every student in that auditorium breathed a sigh of relief, knowing that there would be times when, in spite of our best efforts to develop our own outline, we might have to rely on someone else's. Whenever I have done so, I hope I have given credit where credit is due.

"There is nothing new under the sun" (Ecclesiastes 1:9). Very few human beings are original thinkers, and in fact as Bible preachers, we don't want to be original; we want to be faithful to God's original work. And after 2,000 years of the greatest minds in history pondering the same texts, it is inevitable that we are going to have to use some of their ideas. I once asked my friend Dr. Harold Bussell, then pastor of the First Congregational Church of Hamilton, Massachusetts, and the chaplain of Gordon College, where he got ideas for his sermons. From John Calvin's sermons, he answered. Dr. Bussell was of French-Swiss descent and could read Calvin in the original French. I then asked him where he thought Calvin got his ideas. From Augustine. I then asked him where he thought Augustine got his ideas. "Augustine was original," he said. So unless you are an Augustine, you are going to have to borrow from others. I like to say, "I milk a lot of cows, but I churn my own butter." Draw from a variety of sources, but in the end, make sure your message is truly yours. It is a matter of life and death.

IMPROVING YOUR PREACHING

Be Curious and Interesting

Jim Rayburn, the founder of Young Life, once declared, "It is a sin to bore a kid with the gospel." The gospel of Jesus Christ is the most compelling drama the world has ever heard. What a shame to bore people with our telling of it. Our people confer such an honor upon us each week as they come to church and sit silently listening to us. We should never take that for granted. It is mind-boggling to consider that with all of the forms of communication available, a person standing in front of us and speaking to us is still the most powerful. As J. Kent Edwards points out, this is why politicians try to speak in public to as many people as they possibly can. Television and radio ads have their place, but they are no substitute for the candidate actually speaking to and meeting as many people as he or she possibly can. The preacher standing and speaking to the gathered flock is compelling because the people know him or her. They know that this person is a real human being with abilities and liabilities. They know the family, and they see their pastor in a variety of circumstances in the course of a week. They get to see him or her ministering in times of joy or sorrow. The pastor is a real person, with a real personality, that this church has chosen to be their shepherd. Given the enormity of this honor, it behooves a pastor to be ever growing and learning. Read widely, listen to others' sermons, take courses as you are able.

The wonderful thing is that, even if we can't spend as much time in the library as we want, we can grow and learn in natural, enjoyable ways. When our children were young, we planned a family road trip each summer, limited only by a pastor's salary. Recently when we were with our adult children, they reminded us of the road trips of their childhood. We spent a lot of time exploring museums, historical sites, and natural wonders. We deliberately didn't go to many theme parks. Not only were these road trips bonding times (with the usual sibling quarrels), but they also expanded our horizons, increased our knowledge of the world, and supplied me with many sermon stories and illustrations.

Become a student of the Bible's culture, history, and geography. In my opinion, the best way to do this is to visit the Holy Land. Actually visiting the Bible sites will give you confidence as you describe the geography and history of biblical events. It is not as costly as you might expect, especially if you can recruit others to journey with you. Also, become a student of Western culture and civilization; it is our culture, and it the culture that God chose to spread his message to the world. Reinhold Niebuhr famously said that a pastor should study each day with a Bible in one hand and a newspaper in the other. So read a newspaper, or be otherwise updated on world events and dynamics. Read the great books of our civilization. Have a movie night with your children when you watch well-known film classics. By understanding the world that we and our people live in, we can better communicate with them.

The sermon that the Apostle Paul preached on Mars Hill in Athens (Acts 17) is a wonderful example of understanding the culture of an audience. He speaks to the Athenian culture by quoting from two Greek poets. He addresses their scientific and historical questions, such as the origin of life, the meaning of history, geography, and the motion of everything. He gains a hearing by speaking to the great issues of the day, and then he points them to the risen Christ as the answer. Your people are also curious about the world. They watch national and world news, the History Channel, science channels, travel channels, business channels, and political commentary. They want to know how Jesus Christ and the Bible relate to all of the questions and issues that concern them and their children. We get to show them week after week how Jesus Christ is THE answer to every deep and searching question of human existence. They are curious and, hopefully, we are too.

Become a Good Storyteller

The Bible is mostly narrative, and Jesus was the best storyteller of all time. Fill your sermons with interesting, and well-told stories. Limit the propositional statements in your sermons; remember you are no longer preaching to your Bible school or seminary professors and classmates. Tell the stories of your own life, but more important tell the stories of the Bible, of history, literature, art, film, music. Your congregation will remember your stories, so make sure they are well connected to the biblical truth you are illustrating.

Preach from the Heart

Harold Ockenga used to urge his students, "Preach only what you have experienced." Identify with the drama and emotions in the Scriptures, and convey those feelings. Communicate your own emotions, without crying too much, and certainly without being angry with your people. Be honest with your own struggles. Paul said if we are going to boast, let us boast in our weaknesses because then God gets the glory, and grace is displayed in our lives. Be as transparent as you can be without getting into the specifics of your struggles. Keep those private.

Work Hard on Application

The application part of your sermon is the big "so what?" Don't omit this key element. Show your congregation what God is calling them to be and do in the text. Help your people apply the message to their lives. This is often the most difficult part of the sermon, but the message is incomplete without it. At the end of each message, I try to list three or four simple applications for the congregation. They are offered as suggestions, not as "thou-shalt or shalt-not" commands about how to apply the word to their lives.

Accept the Fact That You Are Unworthy and Get Over It

Remember, you didn't decide to be a preacher; God drafted you. You are doing this because God has called you. So it's not about you. Don't be prideful when people praise your preaching, and don't become discouraged when you don't get accolades or feel you've done well. God can and will use our weakest efforts for His glory. Don't waste time dwelling on a poorly preached sermon. Certainly don't let it ruin your Sunday or Monday. Learn from your mistakes, and vow to do better next time. You have a lifetime to improve.

10

The Renewal of Mission

This season of church revitalization corresponds with the generative years of a marriage—those years when a couple is raising children, building careers, making a home, and in general living a full and satisfying life. They have come to form a deep trust and bond. They share common goals and are working together in pursuing them. So it is with the fruitful years in the life of a church. These are the years when major conflict is in the past and the pastor has survived it by successfully navigating its turbulent waters.

In declining churches, the mission has been lost. Over time there has been missional drift, usually characterized by the church being inwardly focused, allocating all its resources for the benefit of its members. As Archbishop William Temple once said, "The church is the only institution that exists primarily for the benefit of

119

its non-members." But in declining churches, this is no longer the case.

A sure sign of revitalization in a church is a concern to recover an outward-focused mission. More than anything else, it is the renewal of mission that will lead to the full renewal of a church. At the heart of revitalization is a renewed sense in the congregation of caring for those outside the church. It is not enough for the church to wait for the world to come to it. The attractional model worked in the 1970s, 1980s, and even into the 21st century. Today, though, it is an increasingly vain hope to believe that simply offering dynamic worship services or well-designed programs will draw the nonbelieving world through the doors of the church. Only when the church finds a way to offer real hope and help to real people in a lost world does it rediscover and reclaim its biblical mission. And God will always bless that.

The loss of mission was the case in the small church that I served part-time following my retirement from full-time ministry. Officially, the church leaders, who ranged in age from 60 to 80, declared that they wanted to reach the younger families in the community. In reality, everything they did served their own needs and interests. This is not surprising. It is the hallmark of declined churches. Self-serving activities and protection of the status quo are how a church gets to a declined state in the first place.

In survey after survey in that small church (each previous pastor had them conduct a survey), they listed their friendliness as one of their strongest characteristics. This feature was spoken of again and again as I interviewed for the position. I soon realized that their experience of friendliness was friendliness with one another. When new people showed up from time to time, very few people greeted them. One newcomer was told that he was in the seat of a member and was asked to move; this newcomer did move immediately, right out the front door, and never came back. Another newcomer, a young woman, showed up in jeans and was told that she was dressed inappropriately for church. It was easy to find the funds to maintain the status quo. For instance, thousands were spent on a new organ, but it was a battle to get funding to do a neighborhood Vacation Bible School as an outreach. The committees simply recycled the existing members each year, carefully excluding anyone new. One woman told me she had never been asked to serve in any leadership role, despite the fact that she had attended the church faithfully for more than 20 years. Friendliness was in the experience of those already in, not by anyone still on the outside.

When a church begins to be revitalized, it also begins to rediscover its mission in the community. It begins to reflect the demography of the local community. Whereas before revitalization, the membership is not like the surrounding community but is instead a demographic and cultural island, in revitalization it starts to resemble those who live around it. Whereas before, it was unknown and invisible to the larger community, now it begins to become visible as the members embody Christ and live out their faith.

Pastors must lead the way, modeling this incarnational ministry. Pastors called to revitalize will see and seize the opportunities to live out their faith in their communities and neighborhoods. A pastor with a young family finds opportunities volunteering in his children's schools or sports teams. My wife and I did this when our children were young. Later, I found time to serve our town through Rotary, Kiwanis, and the local merchants association. One of my most enjoyable ministries for 15 years was co-hosting a local access cable show with the Reform rabbi in our community. We were polar opposites theologically and politically but have become lifelong friends. Hardly a week went by without someone stopping me on the street and commenting about the show, sometimes agreeing, sometimes disagreeing with the opinions expressed.

Some of the rural pastors that Overseed works with serve as a volunteer firefighters or paramedics, filling a vital need in their towns. Others serve as chaplains to the police or fire departments; still others serve on school boards or town committees, with some even holding local public office.

When the head of the local Veterans Affairs office would ask me to offer a prayer on Memorial Day, Veterans Day, or the Fourth of July, I always said yes. He later told me that he called on me often because other pastors usually turned him down. Maybe they were too busy or were uncomfortable with what some would call "civil religion." I feel they missed opportunities. I believe this is incarnational theology, in which the "love of Christ compels us" to live out our faith in the community.

The church "scattered" is one of the most important messages a pastor can deliver from the pulpit. If we are truthful, we pastors have to admit that much of our effort is spent trying to get our people to attend and support church activities. I believe it ought to be the opposite. We can encourage our congregations to see the 120 hours per week that they are awake as their primary time for ministry. Encouraging a congregation to discover their individual ministries in their workaday worlds is an important step in mission renewal.

We can recapture some of the most powerful truths of the Protestant Reformation, such as the "priesthood of all believers" ("You are . . . a royal priesthood" [I Peter 2:9]). We need to celebrate the ministries of our people in their homes, their workplaces, and their neighborhoods. We can challenge them to become aware of Christ's presence in their daily lives and thus become aware of the people God has put there. The Reformation also celebrated the family, not the monastery, as the normative arena of Christian formation. We can teach our young parents to see themselves as the primary means of the Christian education of their children and the Sunday school as the secondary means. As members open the doors of their homes for small groups and neighborhood gatherings, they get to use gifts of hospitality. Incarnational theology, theology of work, theology of the family, and of the holiness of all of life, are vital teachings for a pastor who wants to lead his or her congregation to rediscover their mission in the world.

With individual members living out their faith in the local community, the whole church can find ways to best serve that community. As the pastor and leaders pray and ask the hard question—"Would anyone miss our church if it ceased to exist?"—they can discover ways they can become a partner for good in that village, town, or city. A church that is serving the local community is a church that would be missed. The town manager of the large suburban community where my church was located felt he could call on us whenever there was a local need. He did so on one occasion after a local flood had displaced a number of families living in public housing. We rallied a group of members to help them move their flood soaked belongings out and then helped provide new furnishing when the damage was repaired. He said afterward we were the only church out of about 15 in our town that he could count on to help. I thought of the words in Acts 2 describing the activity of the early church in Jerusalem as it functioned and grew. Not only did they devote themselves to the Apostles' teaching, to fellowship, breaking of bread, and prayer, they also shared their worldly resources, thus "enjoying the favor of all the people." Meaning all the people of Jerusalem. We know, of course, that in time that favor would fade, and hostility and persecution against the church would follow. For a season though, as they lived out the life of Christ in Jerusalem, the community noticed and was glad they were there.

Another way a whole church can serve a community is to undertake one or more of the very fruitful ministries that have exploded across denominational lines in recent decades. I am thinking of such ministries as Alpha, Divorce Care, Grief Share, Celebrate Recovery, and MOPS or Mom to Mom, to name some of the better known ones. These ministries have obvious benefits:

1. They are ready-made "cookbook" ministries that do not require originality. Simply follow the recipe. These ministries have been field-tested over many years and in many settings. So it is not necessary to start from scratch and create your own program. No need to reinvent the wheel. However, It *is* important to follow the directions and to utilize the guidance and support that these organizations offer.
2. They meet real felt needs. Every community has many people asking the questions of life that Alpha can answer, or dealing with the wounds of divorce, or wrestling with the power of addiction.
3. They are all rooted in biblical truth.
4. They naturally develop leaders as people are trained and then deployed to serve.
5. They demonstrate the love of Christ to your community in ways that earn the community's respect.
6. They lead people to Christ.
7. They add loyal members to your church because people are naturally drawn to places where they find compassion, healing, and hope.

I am familiar with these ministries, our church having used them, and I can testify that properly led and implemented, they really work.

And finally, natural evangelistic opportunities exist for every church in the form of weddings, baptisms, funerals, and Easter and Christmas services. Pastors must decide if their theology allows them to officiate at the weddings and funerals of nonmembers, in which case these major life events become opportunities to share the good news of Jesus Christ. Other community events, such as town fairs, historical celebrations, and parades, also become opportunities for the whole congregation to connect their faith to their local world.

When a church is involved in caring for its community, sooner or later, some people notice and are drawn to the Lord of the Church. One of the most exciting aspects of pastoral ministry is having our congregations praying for the welfare of the community and then leading them in vital mission to it.

11

The Renewal of Worship

The most visible sign of revitalization is on Sunday mornings as the church gathers for worship. Revitalization will most naturally affect how a congregation worships the living God. In his conversation with a woman of Samaria, Jesus assures us that the outward forms are not what matter, but rather the inward realities of "spirit and truth." As a pastor, your most sacred duty will be to lead the people God has given you into a holy, biblical, and spiritual experience of worship. You must strive to shape the kind of worshipper that Jesus told us the Father seeks. And to do this, you must work to craft a worship experience that is God honoring and life transforming.

It seems that whenever there was revival in ancient Israel or in the history of the church, there was an accompanying renewal of worship. We see this in the Old Testament during the reign of Hezekiah, King of Judah (700 BC), when he reopened the Temple in Jerusalem and reinstituted sacred worship. Revival swept the whole nation, and the people were led away from the evil practices of Hezekiah's wicked father Ahaz (II Chronicles 29-30). It was the renewal of worship that led to the revival of the nation. The same can be seen three generations later during the reign of the boy king Josiah. This time, the revival came as the result of the sudden discovery of a copy of the Hebrew Scriptures buried in the debris of the once-again disused Temple (II Chronicles 34-35). It was a dramatic moment when Josiah heard the Word of God for the first time and realized that neglecting it was the reason why the whole nation was under a curse. Once again worship was restored to its central place in the life of Israel, and the nation was revived.

It seems that throughout Christian history worship renewal was always at the center of spiritual revival. This was true in the Reformation and the Great Awakenings in Great Britain and the United States. These events resulted in a huge outpouring of new hymns and other worship forms.

It makes sense that when a local church begins to be revitalized, there will be a desire to see worship renewed as well. Far more important than the outward changes in a worship service will be the inward changes that occur as pastor and congregation determine in their heart to glorify God. A good starting point in renewal of worship would be to preach and teach about worship. As you study, pray, and listen, you will begin to develop what I call a philosophy of worship. It will shape the form and meaning worship will take in your particular congregation.

It is very tempting to begin changing the worship service to suit your personal tastes or the perceived tastes of the demographic you hope to reach, usually younger. Unilaterally making sudden, drastic changes, or even minor changes, to the worship service is a guaranteed way to start what Gordon MacDonald calls the "worship wars." Until a congregation has given the pastor freedom to make changes, a better place to start is by developing your theology or your philosophy of worship.

In developing a philosophy of worship, we must start with God. It is God who always takes the initiative in the Divine-

Human relationship, and worship is our response. The very word "worship" comes into English from the Anglo-Saxon word *weorthscipe*, which means to assign worth to something (Martin, p. 10). To worship God means to give him the ultimate worth that He alone is due. All of Christian worship is a response to God, whether it is in songs of praise, prayers of petition, Holy Communion, the collecting of offerings, or preaching and hearing the Word. Worship is the Christian's response to everything that God has done, not just in our personal lives but throughout salvation history. It starts with God's first act of Creation declared in Genesis and continues with the salvation of Noah through the flood, which Peter saw as a symbol of baptism in Christ (I Peter 3:19-21). Salvation history really gets rolling with the call of Abraham, and the rest of the Bible is the story of this one man and his descendants—especially his most important descendant, Jesus.

All of the Old Testament's twists and turns in the journey of the Hebrew people were preparation for the coming of Jesus Christ. His suffering, death, and resurrection are the culmination of salvation history. This saving history is then carried forward by the Holy Spirit in the work of the Church in the world down through human history. It will achieve its fulfillment in the return of Christ and the coming of His kingdom. This is the story preachers get to tell in worship each week, and all of our worship is our "Yes" to God for His loving and saving action on our behalf. As Paul declares in II Corinthians 1:19, "for the Son of God, Jesus Christ, who was preached among you . . . was not 'Yes' and 'No' but in Him it has always been 'Yes.'" Try as the ancient Israelites did to obey the Law, they were never able to make a total response of "Yes" to God. Because of the redeeming work of Jesus Christ, all who believe *are* able to respond with wholehearted worship to God. As a renewal pastor reads, studies, and preaches the whole saving history of God, he or she will lay a foundation for a philosophy of worship.

A VERY BRIEF HISTORY OF WORSHIP

Fortunately for us, archaeologists have never unearthed a Sunday worship bulletin from a first-century worship service. Otherwise, Christians would have been tempted to slavishly reproduce it week after week for two millennia. Worship is too dynamic for that. However, archaeologists and biblical historians can help us understand the essential framework of early Christian worship.

Jewish Influence in Early Christian Worship

The very first church at Jerusalem began its existence within the family of Judaism. First-century Roman and Jewish authorities considered the Christians as a sect of Judaism. The first Christians, however, were radically distinguished by their total confidence that Jesus was the Messiah of Israel. Nevertheless, they were shaped in their worship practices by Jewish worship in the Temple in Jerusalem and later by Jewish synagogue worship in the diaspora. Acts 2 tells us of the church's participation in the Temple worship, though certainly without involvement in the animal sacrifices because Jesus had already reinterpreted that component for them in the Last Supper. The Christians added to Temple worship their unique practices of gathering for the Apostles' teaching and for the "breaking of bread," which was a combination of the agape feast and the Lord's Supper.

When the church moved beyond Jerusalem and drew into its fold Hellenistic Jews and gentile proselytes, it was shaped more by the synagogue experience of these individuals. The synagogue service consisted of hymns of praise, the reading of the Scriptures, the expounding of Scriptures, and prayers of petition for God's blessing. Early Jewish documents, the Dead Sea scrolls, the Gospels, and the letters of Paul all shed light on this synagogue influence on early Christian worship. Further understanding of this can be found in New Testament scholar Ralph P. Martin's *Worship in the Early Church*.

129

A Four-fold Pattern of Worship

What emerges from these roots of Christian worship is a pattern that has shaped Christian worship from the first century until today. If you *could* unearth a first-century church bulletin, it would reveal a three-fold worship pattern of Praise, Word, and Response. Robert Webber, in his 1998 book *Planning Blended Worship: The Creative Mixture of Old and New*, expands this basic three-part structure into four parts:

1. ***Gathering,*** which includes praise among other things. The Gathering is the entrance of God's people into the presence of God. The congregation symbolically enters the presence of the living God the same way the ancient Jewish people entered the Temple courts in Jerusalem where the manifest presence of God resided. Whenever ancient Israel gathered in the Temple, they expected to be in the presence of God. Jesus told His followers to expect His presence when they gathered en masse. The writer of Hebrews warns believers not to neglect gathering together for worship. While individual worship is to be a daily life style for the believer, it is in corporate, gathered worship that we can expect to most fully experience the living Christ. While the Gathering involves a number of elements, the chief one is praise. We enter His gates with thanksgiving and His courts with praise.

2. ***Word,*** which includes the reading of God's word and then the instructing of the people from that Word. Although this has taken different forms down through Christian history, these two aspects—reading and preaching—are the essence of this part of worship.

3. ***Thanksgiving*** is the response to God's Word out of gratitude. It includes the Lord's Supper, the giving and collecting of offerings, and the peoples' prayers of thanks and petition.

4. ***Dismissal*** is the final act of Sunday worship. It brings the
   service to a close, and through a word of blessing or
   benediction, it reminds the congregation that the believers'
   whole life is an act of worship (Romans 12:1). As
   congregants leave the house of worship, they present their
   whole selves for the coming week as a living sacrifice to
   God. And that is their truest worship.

All four aspects are a response to God and form a framework
onto which each major Christian tradition—Roman, Eastern, and
Protestant—has been able construct a sound biblical, spiritual, and
historical theology of worship. Let's look a little closer at each part
of this worship pattern.

1. The Gathering

As we think about the first part of this four-part theology of
worship, we should keep in mind two primary realities. The first is
that God is drawing worshippers to Himself. In John 4:23 Jesus
redirects the Samaritan woman's thinking away from the cultural
particulars of worship, such as the location of the sacred mountain,
to the universal fact of holy worship, namely that God is actively
seeking "true" worshippers. When you think about the worship
service that you are planning for the coming Sunday, keep in mind
that God is way ahead of you in planning. He is already speaking
to the hearts of people, drawing them to Himself. He is actively
calling people to worship Him, and some of them will be gathering
at your church on Sunday. In planning worship you are
cooperating with God in fashioning a worship experience that will
draw in those worshippers He is seeking. We should never be
surprised when people show up on Sunday morning whom we
would least expect. It is not our polished preaching or our skilled
music that is bringing them; it is the Lord.

The second thing to keep in mind is that many people come
through the doors of your sanctuary hungry for a "thus says the
Lord" experience. They show up for as many reasons as there are

people, but for many if not most, it is out of a yearning for an experience with the living Lord. They are weary from having walked in the world all week. They are sad from the broken relationships that they live with. They are ashamed and feeling guilty for their sins. They are lonely, lost, and afraid. Even so, or just because, God has graciously drawn them to your church. Everything we do to prepare for the Gathering is sacred work. It is so important that the pastor and the worship leaders think through every aspect of this first part of the worship framework. Think about your website and what it says to help make people feel safe in attending your church. Consider such mundane things as convenient parking, building signage, accessibility, greeters who can direct newcomers to the right place. Take a look at the cleanliness of your building, especially your restrooms and children's spaces. Think about lighting and an open, uncluttered entry area. It is all sacred because God is using this space to draw true worshippers to Himself.

Music preludes help set the tone for what is to come. This is not just filler music until the real action of worship starts, but it begins the process of drawing people into the presence of God. The revitalization of worship will require pastors and their leaders to make tough decisions about worship music, and it starts with the preludes.

The Gathering "officially" begins with a spoken **Welcome and Greeting**. Until you have trained other people to give the opening welcome and greeting, you should take this duty on yourself. It should be thought through carefully, conveying a sense of grace and love, and all the while, it should be concise and not rambling.

Announcements, in my opinion, should come next. They are a necessary but not terribly important part of the whole Gathering. Again, until you have trained others to make the announcements, you should do them yourself for the sake of clarity and brevity. Develop your own rationale for what gets announced.

Mine came about as a result of visiting a colleague's church many years ago one Sunday while on vacation. I was very tired, spiritually empty, and hungry for an encounter with the Lord. The service started well with some uplifting worship music. Then it ground to a halt as my friend made a few announcements then invited the members of this small congregation to offer any announcements of their own. One dear woman stood up and made what was probably a 5-minute announcement about the church's food pantry. My spirit groaned within me, and from my vantage point in the back of the sanctuary, I could see that the rest of the congregation was rapidly tuning out. For me, it felt like an "Ichabod" moment when the Spirit departed from the Temple. It felt as though sacred worship had just been hijacked and trivialized. I immediately thought of times when I had done the same thing. I vowed then to establish a protocol for announcements. With my Elders we decided that all announcements would be printed in the bulletin (later on the website or scrolled on a screen beforehand) and the church's attention directed there. Any announcements given from the pulpit would have to be very important and would apply to the whole congregation, not particular groups or ministries. And they would be very brief. When an announcement had to be made by someone else, I always held the microphone. This is a lesson I learned from the very wise and gifted pastor Gordon MacDonald. This way, you will never subject your God-hungry flock to a long-winded announcement about minor matters. In my experience, the majority of church announcements are ignored by the majority of the congregation and are therefore mostly ineffective.

The **Call to Worship** and an **Opening Prayer** can follow the Welcome and Greeting. This call and prayer should convey, in whatever words you choose, the strong convictions we have as Christians that it is God who has called us together for the sacred task of worshipping Him and to receive from Him grace and blessing. This should never be rote formality, or casual glibness, but carefully articulated.

Worship Music is the real substance of the Gathering. This is the time of praise, adoration, and thanksgiving to the Lord. (I will elaborate on music in worship in a later section in this chapter.) Suffice it to say, it is this part of a worship service that ushers God's people into the experience of God's presence. Because of the very sacred nature of this part of worship, a pastor can expect it to ignite his or her greatest battles in church revitalization, the so-called "worship wars." If this part of worship were not so important, we would not encounter the conflict that we often do. It is not an exaggeration to say that in some cases this battle may even be spiritual warfare. As responsible shepherds we might have to stand up like Moses and say to controlling powers, human or spiritual, "Thus says the Lord, 'Let my people go, that they may worship me.'"

The purpose of Worship Music is to bring the people into God's presence and prepare them to hear God's Word, which is the next part in the pattern.

2. The Word

In some churches, the Word often includes a Children's Message. Including children in the early part of the service is important as they get to they see their parents and other adults worshipping. While there are many ways to do a children's message, the best I ever came across was a "mystery box." We called it the Good News Mystery Box. It was simply a covered, opaque plastic container that was given to a randomly chosen child each month. (We did a children's talk once a month, not weekly.) The child would then bring the box back to church the following month, having put into it any object they wanted that would fit, live animals excepted. Neither I nor anyone else but the parents knew what was inside. With all the kids gathered around me at the front, I would open the box and give an impromptu children's talk based on the object. It is not as hard as it seems, and even when the talk didn't go so well, the children and adults enjoyed seeing me flounder. It was fun, I didn't have to prepare anything in advance, and who doesn't like a surprise? I chose to do the mystery box myself each month, not because there weren't others who could do it, but because it was important for me as pastor to know these youngest disciples in my flock. And the parents wanted their children to know me, as well.

Meet and Greet. During the transition time in the service while the children were leaving for Sunday school, we would invite the congregation to stand where they were and greet those around them in the love of Christ. This was our version of the "passing of the peace." Because we had many formerly unchurched members, this informal option seemed a more natural way to "pass the peace." It accomplished the same purpose in a more colloquial way. It was simply to demonstrate that a congregation is a body of believers, not a collection of individuals. Obviously real Christian community cannot be established in a 30-second meet and greet; small groups are the only really effective way to build a deeper Christian community.

After greeting one another and being seated, the congregation's attention can be drawn to the **Public Reading of the Word**. Unfortunately, the public reading and hearing of Scripture has disappeared from many contemporary churches. In the process, they have lost a basic element of Christian worship that goes all the way back to the Church's roots in the ancient Jewish synagogue. The New Testament includes several instances of the public reading of the Scriptures in the synagogues. One instance is Luke 4:16-22, where Jesus reads from Isaiah in his home synagogue in Nazareth and then gives the sermon. Another is in Acts 13:15-16, where the synagogue rulers did the reading then invited Paul to give the sermon. It is also evident from various epistles (Colossians, I Thessalonians, Philemon) that the Apostle Paul expected his letters to be read publicly and shared in this way.

The custom of the public reading of the Scriptures in the Jewish synagogue was deemed so vital a part of worship by the Apostles that it naturally carried over into the first-century church. Paul exhorts Timothy to "devote himself to the public reading of scripture" (I Timothy 4:13). New Testament scholar Ralph P. Martin describes the public reading of scripture as "an inheritance we have received, through the early church, from the worship (experience) of Judaism" (p. 69).

Later on in church history, in the 1500s, Martin Luther translated the Bible into German so that it could be understood as it was read publically in worship services, rather than in Latin, as was the custom in the Roman church. It was not until the 1960s that the Roman Catholic Church ordered the Bible to be read publicly in the vernacular.

Given today's technologies, there are many ways that a congregation can follow along with the reading, including of course in their own or the church's pew Bibles, but the reading of scripture in public worship should never be neglected. As with other public speaking aspects of worship, a pastor should carefully choose and train people to read the Scripture lessons.

Preaching is the culmination of the ministry of the Word section of worship. It is safe to say that preaching is the "center of gravity" in Christian worship (Martin, p. 69). Chapter 9 was devoted exclusively to the sacred work of preaching and its chief place in Christian worship. In ancient Jewish and Christian worship, the sermon was not the final element. Instead, the response to the preached Word came after the sermon. Putting the sermon at the end of the service is a late evangelical Protestant tradition, not an early Christian one.

3. Thanksgiving

Thanksgiving, the third part of the worship framework, is the response by the people to the Word of God. To be honest, we preachers too often focus our preaching on what we want our people to do for God, but the best biblical preaching focuses first on what God has done and is doing for us. If we have been faithfully proclaiming the narrative of God's redemptive acts on our behalf, then a thankful response is always appropriate. The following are elements of worship that have historically been included in this part of worship.

Public Prayer, in traditional Congregational churches like the one I grew up in, was usually called the pastoral prayer. Frequently, public prayer is a very long, tedious, and formulaic prayer offered by the pastor. Sometimes it is a recap of the sermon, perhaps betraying some lingering doubt about the effectiveness of the sermon. Typically, this public prayer is petitionary in nature, but too often it dwells exclusively on the peculiar needs of the local congregation and their extended family. There are many helpful frameworks for prayer. In my ministry, through the encouragement of an Episcopal friend, I eventually settled on the Book of Common Prayer to guide my public prayer. The outline I used lifts up four areas of need: (1) our church, its ministries and leaders, as well as neighboring churches and the church worldwide, including our missionaries and the persecuted church; (2) the nations of the world, "kings and all those in authority" (I Timothy 2:2), being mindful of such issues as natural disasters and political turmoil; (3) individuals who are afflicted or troubled in any way, mentioning both general categories and individuals, by names if appropriate; and (4) those who don't know Christ or who have lost their faith. Such a prayer addresses personal needs weighing on the hearts of our people but also moves beyond the narrow interests of the local congregation to the broader needs of the world. A pastor or layperson offering the public prayer can easily adapt this format to the particular needs and concerns of the congregation.

In smaller churches, the prayer leader can invite prayer requests from the congregation, but with certain guidelines to keep the process from being dominated by a few. Many churches have a team of trained laypeople who are available following the service to offer personal prayer for those who desire it. This is a good ministry for pastors to give away so they are available to the whole congregation after the service.

The recitation of **the Lord's Prayer** has been an integral part of Christian worship since the end of the first century (Martin, p. 35). In the twenty-first century, many churches no longer recite it, perhaps because it is viewed as a rote exercise done in a mindless manner. Better than eliminating it would be to do some teaching on it, and on prayer in general, and then find ways to more creatively include it. The Lord's Prayer is still the most incredible prayer ever uttered due to the comprehensiveness of the subjects covered, the beauty of its language, and its brevity. If nothing else it is a good model for pastors to emulate in their own public prayers. And it signals to visitors unfamiliar with what your church believes that you are part of the Church universal.

Reciting Creeds also belongs in this part of the service. Depending on your church's tradition, this may be a weekly or periodic part of the service. A creed such as the Apostles' Creed is a touchstone for a church and declares succinctly and eloquently what it believes and teaches.

The giving and collecting of **Offerings** is an important part of the people's response to worship, not just a necessity to be done in a perfunctory way. In the offering we recognize many things, including God's gracious provision of work and the opportunity to acquire and use material wealth. We also understand our giving as an antidote to the danger that money poses. Further, we recognize all of life as a gift to be stewarded for the Lord. And finally, our giving is an opportunity to bless others with the whole ministry of the church. The church that we now attend invites the congregation to bring their offerings forward and place them in a basket. I believe this active participation by the congregation aptly symbolizes the offering as a response to God's goodness.

The Lord's Supper is the last component in the Thanksgiving/Response part of worship. This is not the place to discuss the diverse views of communion, but suffice it to say that each pastor should be conversant with the beliefs of his or her church tradition and the liturgy involved in celebrating it. In independent and free (Congregational and Baptist) churches, there is wider latitude in those beliefs and in the forms the celebration of communion takes. Early on in my Congregational church pastorate, communion was celebrated in typical Protestant fashion with deacons distributing the elements to a seated congregation. As the church grew and we added a second service, we had difficulty recruiting enough deacons to serve communion at both. One day, a new member of the church suggested we do what they did in the Lutheran church he grew up in: have the congregation come forward to receive the elements from just two servers, me and one deacon. I did a little research and found that our existing practice of distribution did not date from time immemorial but came about in the 19th century during epidemics of contagious diseases. Churches abandoned the practice of a common cup for fear of contracting infections in favor of individual served cups. Many of the oldest New England Congregational churches still possess valuable antique silver communion chalices that were the common cups for communion. Because my leaders were reluctant to make such a radical move for both services, we implemented the new format only in the second service. It was an immediate success and we soon adopted the practice in the first service, too.

What started out for us simply as a convenience became a very moving worship experience. It was not uncommon for people to make their way forward with tears streaming down their face. The symbolism of coming to the Lord was powerful. Those of us who got to stand at the front and offer the elements in Christ's name were also deeply moved. We eventually allowed elders and staff this privilege. Sometimes we offered prayers of healing during communion. Other times on communion Sundays I might give an invitation to receive Christ as Lord and Savior and then use the symbolism of coming to the Lord's table to help people visualize the act. Our church could never go back to the historically recent and more passive form of distribution to a seated congregation. But whatever form and meaning your particular service of communion takes, be sure to give this sacred act enough time in the service. It is not something to be rushed.

4. Dismissal
In the Gospels of Matthew and Mark, the Last Supper concludes with Jesus and his disciples **Singing a Hymn** and then leaving the upper room. Concluding a service with a hymn is an ancient tradition in Christian worship. It may be a praise song reprised from earlier in the service to remind the congregation of the theme of the message. It could also be a bright, upbeat hymn that sends the congregation out on a stirring note. Like all worship music, it should be melodic and singable because it is the last song parishioners will take from the service.

The **Benediction** is the final act of the Dismissal. The benediction is not a prayer; it is a pronouncement of God's blessing on the people as they depart the church and go out into the world. It says that although this part of our worship is over, the most sacred part of our worship has just begun—the presenting of our whole selves as a living sacrifice to Christ—and that this is our "spiritual" worship (Romans 12:1). A closing prayer is not needed; a brief reminder of God's present strength with us all week is enough.

DEVELOPING A PHILOSOPHY OF WORSHIP
Renewing worship is neither haphazard nor hurried nor wholesale. As I said at the start of this chapter, worship renewal should be shaped by your philosophy of worship—so if you haven't done so already, develop one. Great patience and prayer are required

because worship is the most potent aspect of church's life. Getting worship "right" is not only the most important but also the most challenging task of revitalization. Introducing change in the way a church worships will invariably produce the most resistance and conflict. And revitalized worship will also produce the most fruit in the life of a church. It is through worship, with solid preaching at its heart, that the work of evangelism happens best. Faithful biblical preaching and vital worship will inevitably draw people to Christ and transform lives. The Book of Revelation reminds us we will spend eternity in endless praise and worship to the Lamb, so a little practice now is worth it.

Here are a few practical pointers to keep in mind as you develop the philosophy of worship that will guide your worship renewal.

1. Do not neglect prayer and Scripture study. A good place to begin is by journeying together with your elders or deacons so that a philosophy emerges in the collective wisdom of God's people.
2. Teach about worship from the pulpit.
3. Recruit a prayer team to uphold Sunday worship each week.
4. Focus on small but significant changes, and always prepare your congregation for the changes in advance.
5. Decide if your worship is directed more to believers or seekers (ideally, both), and then assess its effectiveness in ministering to each group.
6. Consider how easy it is for visitors or newcomers to understand and participate in worship at your church. Are there elements that are confusing or exclusive? Are there elements that are specifically welcoming to "outsiders"? Aim for barrier-free worship.
7. Set up "secret shoppers"—trusted visitors to evaluate your worship service in light of your philosophy.

8. Strive to eliminate anything that trivializes worship and to increase the sense of holy awe.
9. Work to increase the congregation's participation, for example, with singing, responses, unison reading of Scripture, actively bringing offerings forward or coming to the Table for communion, kneeling or standing for prayer. Worship is not a spectator sport; help your people offer themselves in worship.
10. Use the worship gifts and resources you currently have, but pray for God to raise up more.

A word on the length of worship services. A church experiencing renewal often sees the length of the worship service creep upward. There may be pressure to add more praise music, or introduce drama, or extend prayer time. The multiplication of ministries means more groups want their activities announced or promoted. Simply having more people attending will increase the time needed to do everything.

What I have observed is that as a service expands beyond 75 to 90 minutes, attendance begins to level off and even decline. This is not a scientific observation, just anecdotal. If you advertise your services as an hour, then strive to maintain that length. If a church grows to need multiple services, it will be imperative to keep to time limits because of overlapping parking needs. By sticking to stated time limits, you also show respect to Sunday school teachers and nursery workers who care for the children of the church. There will always be the gung-ho enthusiasts who want more, and they will accuse you of limiting God to a schedule. You can simply remind them that God is eternal; we are the ones who have limits, and we have to live within them.

WORSHIP MUSIC

Sing a new song! Renewal of worship music almost always includes " singing a new song." Psalm 149:1, Isaiah 42:10, Revelations 5:9 all tell us to sing a "new song," probably because songs grow old very fast. Few songs or music styles last very long. There are some that do, of course. At Christmas, we sing "Of the Father's Love Begotten," which was written by Prudentius in the 4th century! Many of the hymns of the Reformation or the Great Awakenings are still as fresh as the day they were written in the 16th, 17th, 18th and 19th centuries. The prime example is "Amazing Grace." That said, the vast majority of songs written in the past belong in the past. The worship of the Holy God needs fresh expression in each generation.

Be culturally appropriate in the style of music you are introducing. After a few months, you have a good idea of the makeup of your congregation. The age of the congregation is not necessarily the most important factor in whether certain music styles will be accepted. More important is the music experience of the people. If you have younger people who were raised in a traditional hymn-singing congregation, they may resist contemporary music more than aging boomers who were never part of a church but grew up on rock and roll. Ask yourself what is appropriate for your people. This is the argument that the Apostle Paul makes in I Corinthians 14:23-25 when he discusses tongues speaking in the local church. He tells what will happen when unbelievers come into the church and there is no one to interpret the message: the outsider will hear the "babble" of tongues and conclude the people are out of their minds. Paul is not against speaking in tongues, but he exhorts that it be done in a way that is culturally fitting. What is appropriate in one setting may be jarring in another. For instance, I have sat at Fenway Park in Boston on many occasions and witnessed the whole ballpark swelling in a late-inning wave to rally the Red Sox. It is great fun! But trying to start a wave when you are at a classical concert in Boston's

Symphony Hall will get you ushered out in a hurry. In the same way, introducing electric guitars and drums to a congregation steeped in hymns and organ music is going to be equally jarring. This is not to say don't do it, but do understand the process and the timing involved. Also, be culturally appropriate for the demographics you are trying to reach. If you are trying to reach a younger age group, the music will have to be more contemporary.

Strive for excellence. We should seek excellence in everything we do, for we serve an excellent Lord and excellence honors God and builds confidence in people. My advice is that you not introduce major change in worship until you have the musicians and leadership needed to pull it off. Badly done worship music is jarring, like fingernails on a chalkboard. People will tolerate something more willingly if it is done well. If your music pool is inadequate, try borrowing some worship leaders and musicians from a sister church with an abundance of them. Many larger churches have a deep bench of musicians and are willing to loan out a team to help jump-start contemporary music in a declining church. My church, which was rich in music gifts, loaned our second team to another church for two years to help build their music team. Whereas it might take years to randomly accumulate the leadership necessary to form a high-quality worship band, one borrowed for a season can accelerate the whole transition. They can train your leaders, and model for the congregation what a blended or contemporary service might look like.

Know that God is the audience in worship. The 18th century Danish philosopher Soren Kierkegaard reminded us that Christian worship is like a drama, with an Audience, Actors, and a Prompter. This is a profound analogy. We often get it wrong and think of the preacher and worship leaders as the actors, the congregation as the audience, and God as the prompter, inspiring preacher and musicians to get their parts right. It's just the opposite. God is our audience. It is before Him that we live out our lives. The congregation are the actors, striving to play their parts in obedience to His call. The preacher and musicians are the prompters, encouraging the congregation to play their parts in the whole scheme of things. If pastor and musicians can keep this truth in mind, they can resist pressure from the congregation and their egos to turn Sunday worship into a performance. Every pastor feels the pressure to preach to the congregation's expectations. It is liberating to know the only audience you have is God. He alone truly knows your effort and intent, and in the end, He is the only one you have to please.

Congregational worship is about the congregation, not the leader. There is a false theology that says, "If the congregation can just see how fervent the worship leaders are, they will be inspired to worship." It's a false theology because, as Kierkegaard observed, worship is not about what the leader or leaders are doing, it is about what the congregation is doing. The personal worship experience of the leader, expressed for example with closed eyes and raised hands, is secondary to that of the congregation. The greatest act of worship for the worship leader is to help usher the congregation into the holy presence of God. Like John the Baptist, they become lesser as He becomes greater.

The same goes for lengthy comments by a worship leader about a song or what it means to them. These are useful *only* if they truly help the congregation engage in worship. The only comments by a music leader should be to guide the congregation in singing the song. Songs speak for themselves; they do not need a commentary from the leader. Usually a simple introduction is enough, or in most cases too much. Remember, preachers preach and worship leaders lead worship.

Here are some practical musical notes learned from years of experience in both leading worship and sitting in the congregation:

- Because the worship leader is leading the whole congregation, he or she should lead from a prominent, visible place and be heard above the other musicians and the instruments. And the leader should sing the melody line, not harmonize, if he or she expects the congregation to do likewise. This is especially true when introducing a new song.

- Songs must be singable first and theologically sound second. Ideally both, but if you have to choose, it makes no sense to have a doctrinally correct song that no one can sing. Songs should also be sung in a key that most people can comfortably reach.

- Introduce new songs at a rate at which people can learn them. One new song a month is a pace I have found do-able. Sing the new song a couple of times in a month, then continue to sing it through the year as you add to the repertoire. It often takes singing a song many times until people are comfortable with it and begin to like it. And it doesn't become part of their worship until it is in their hearts.

- Control the volume. There is often a tug of war between a pastor and the worship leader over the volume of the music. If people cannot hear themselves sing, they will stop singing, in which case they have stopped worshiping. Remember the goal is to have the congregation sing, the volume must foster that.

Renewing worship is especially difficult because (1) there are so many moving parts to coordinate and (2) everyone has strong opinions about worship and music. Worship wars are common while you are trying to get this sorted out. It is a continually moving target, and you are always aware that you can do a better job. But because we are talking about the worship of the Holy God, it is worth every effort. A helpful book to read together as a leadership team is Gordon MacDonald's *Who Stole My Church?* The title alone is a hint to the high emotional stakes and the entrenched ownership the congregation feels toward worship.

Good worship music is second only to preaching the Word of God in the process of church renewal. Thom Rainer cites a study on the reasons people choose a church. The top reason for 83 percent is the quality of the sermons, while for 74 percent it is the style of the worship music. That's why I suggest that the second most important staff/leadership position to fill after the senior pastor is the worship/music leader. If you have an opportunity to fill one new position, make it the worship/music director. It is unfortunate that pastors and church boards hire administrators, associate pastors, custodians, organists, choir directors, treasurers, or bookkeepers before they hire worship directors.

In small churches with limited finances, a volunteer from the congregation may be the only option. An advantage is that this person is likely to already have the trust and support of the congregation. If an internal volunteer is not an option and the funds are there, make the effort to find the right person. In most small to medium size churches, this is a part-time job because there simply is not enough work to keep a full-time worship director busy. Avoid the temptation to try to create a full-time job by bundling together several disparate jobs such as children's minister/worship director because people will always favor their gifts and work to their strengths, neglecting the other part of the job. But if a full-time salary is the only way to entice the right worship leader, then allow them to play to their strengths and find volunteers to assist with other parts of the job.

Often the best candidates for this position are second-tier leaders or musicians from larger churches in the area. Typically, they are volunteers in those larger churches and have gained experience working in that setting. When they are given the opportunity to actually earn income while serving God according to their gifts, most will jump at the opportunity. One of the best worship directors we ever had was a very talented man who came to us from a church in the same community. When we posted the position, he approached us. In that other church, he was receiving only a small stipend for his services, and he was working full-time as a secretary elsewhere to support his family. When we offered him a full-time job as our director of worship, he was thrilled. As soon as he told his board that he was leaving, I received a phone call from a very angry chairman, who accused me of plundering his church. He warned that he was going to write a letter to my board to complain. I simply asked him if he worked full time and was paid accordingly. Yes, of course. Then, why he would deny that opportunity to his brother in Christ? He had no answer but still managed to grumble as he hung up. He never did send a letter.

Enfold the worship leaders into the life of the church. It is too easy to isolate them as performers who do their thing on Sunday morning and then stand apart from the rest of the life of the church. They should be involved in the community and mission of the church. Their leadership authority is enhanced as worship leaders know and care for the congregation.

Maintain a close supportive relationship with the music leaders. Godly, talented music leaders are precious commodities, and you should affirm them, support them, and especially protect them from criticism. Recognize that effective, God-honoring worship takes time to research, select, arrange, orchestrate, and rehearse, so give your worship leaders the time, resources, and encouragement they need. The experience of true Christian community in a church begins when those in leadership positions are living and working in harmony, and it then flows outward to the congregation.

BLENDED WORSHIP

I clearly recall the moment when, as a young pastor in an aging congregation, God spoke to me about worship music and how important it was in reaching my generation for Christ. It is true that God speaks in strange ways. I was in the car late one night driving to join my wife and children on vacation at our camp in Maine. To stay awake I was listening to a syndicated rock and roll radio station, singing along with all of the songs of my youth. It struck me how much I enjoyed that music (I have long since switched to classical music as my favorite genre). My next thought was how out-of-sync the music in our church was for my generation. I realized that if we were going to reach my generation, we would have to make a music shift. That "revelation" began a long, slow, and often awkward process of blending contemporary music into our worship service. Every generation is strongly and emotionally connected to its music, and so worship music must speak to the generation a church is trying to reach. Each generation and culture has the right to hear the gospel in its own language, and that includes its own music.

With that in mind, as you reshape worship, choose the music style that your congregation listens to most on the radio. Is it pop, country, gospel, classical, choral, organ? Martin Luther understood this notion 400 years before the invention of radio. He chose tunes sung in the beer halls of Germany and assigned Christian lyrics to them. He famously said, "Why should the devil have all the good music?"

Contemporary music is the most widely disseminated form of music. Wherever Western culture has gone, it has introduced rock and roll and all its iterations. It makes no sense for congregations to revert exclusively to 18th, 19th, and early 20th century music forms such as hymns and gospel songs on Sundays when they listen to contemporary music forms the rest of the week. Virtually everyone alive in America today has spent their entire lives listening to pop music. The oldest boomers, now in their 70s, cut their musical teeth on rock and roll. Even praise music is now 60 years old, having first emerged from the 1960s folk mass scene. Contemporary music is no longer a new thing, and churches need to find a way to incorporate it in worship, if they have not done so already.

Unfortunately, it sometimes seems that the only way to update worship in a very traditional church is to add a contemporary service. I know pastors who, out of frustration, are tempted to do an end run around the resistance by starting a second, alternative, contemporary service. If you do decide to add a contemporary or alternative service, do not be in a hurry to do so. Take your time to do this and proceed very cautiously. There are several reasons why I offer this caution. First, two different services can divide the congregation into the "rockers" and the "old fogies." Neither service will reflect the diversity that the Body of Christ is meant to manifest. The miracle of the church is that it overcomes ages, races, economics, and all manner of cultural differences. Having services based on those differences goes against the purposes of God for His church. Second, it is an enormous amount of work to create even one quality worship service each week, let alone two different ones. Few small or medium size churches have the leadership to do it. Third, people generally do not choose their worship service based on the content but on the time of the service. It is a myth to think that if you have an early-morning contemporary service, young members will choose it while elderly people will flock to a later service. The fact is that people choose the worship time based on lifestyle, not musical style. If you do decide to offer a separate contemporary service, then do it on Sunday morning. Services scheduled for off times, such as Saturday night or Sunday afternoon, are usually unsuccessful and eventually scrapped. And in the meantime, you end up burning out staff and volunteers, who now must give up their entire weekend. A separate contemporary service may be the only way forward in worship renewal if trying to change a traditional service proves impossible. But in my opinion it is a last-resort measure.

A far better solution is to strive for blended worship. One style does not fit all. The Church has more than 3,000 years of lyrics to draw on (going back to the Psalms) and 1,000 years of tunes. There are prayers, creeds, and other worship elements that are centuries old. They have stood the test of time and have guided the church in worship for millennia. Pastors and worship leaders should discover the secret of their staying power, rather than simply discarding them. Some of these ancient worship elements are like fine old antiques, still beautiful, useful, and valuable. On the other hand, not everything old is an antique; some old things are just junk to be put out with the trash. Wise pastors and worship leaders are able to distinguish between the trash and the treasures. Blended worship is the most difficult worship style to achieve. It takes skill and practice to achieve. However, done well, there is no more powerful tool for leading the diverse body of Christ into the presence of the Holy God.

Initiating and leading change in your church's worship service may be the most difficult aspect of church revitalization. Start with a well-thought-out, biblical philosophy of worship, and then gently, patiently lead your people into a deeper, richer worship experience.

12

The Renewal of Organization

A pastor involved in church revitalization will quickly realize that the church's organizational structure can be a major factor keeping the church dysfunctional and ineffective in reaching people for Christ. Small, dying churches seem to be religiously devoted to maintaining their organizational structure. Often the bylaws are more revered and more scrupulously studied than the Bible.

For reasons I don't fully understand, declining, dying churches will strive to fill all of the committee positions dictated by their bylaws even if it requires everyone to serve, and many to serve in multiple roles. The first church I served averaged about 70 on a Sunday morning in my early years there, but it took 85 people to fill all of the boards and committees. Decades earlier, the church had numbered about 900 in attendance and the bylaws reflected that. There were two main boards: Trustees who oversaw the property and finances, and Deacons who were responsible for the spiritual life of the church (whatever that meant). There was a Music Committee to oversee the organist and choir director; a

Christian Education Committee that operated a tiny Sunday school; a Missions committee that managed a small mission budget; a Flower Committee; a Fair Committee; a Women's Ministry Committee; a Boy Scout Committee; a Church Supper Committee; and a few others whose names and functions I have forgotten.

THE CHURCH COUNCIL/COMMITTEE SYSTEM

At one time, there had also been an executive committee called the Church Council. It gathered the heads of the various committees together each month to have them report on their activities. My predecessor managed to dissolve the Church Council because of its long history of squabbling and political wrangling. I never fully appreciated what my predecessor had accomplished in terminating the Church Council until I had retired from that church and briefly pastored a small, declining church that had a similar church council system. I soon discovered that it is the church structure from Hades. In this second church, the council was composed of the chair of each committee in the church, plus the officers: Deacons, Trustees, Music Committee, Fair Committee, Children's Committee, the Pastoral Relations Committee, Moderator, Clerk, Treasurer, Superintendent of the Sunday school, Finance Committee, Nominating Committee, Social Committee, Flower Committee, and Outreach Committee. Fifteen people in all, plus me as pastor, and I was the only one who did not have a vote. (It is not uncommon for small churches to have bylaws that restrict the pastor from voting.) Very little got done at these meetings because all the time was spent giving reports and voicing complaints. To make matters worse these meetings, were held on Sunday nights, when everyone would rather have been home with their families. I anticipated those meetings with lots of prayer and an anxious feeling in the pit of my stomach. After a year of trying to lead this dysfunctional church, I resigned in frustration. Even so, I do not regret one moment of that year because a few people were won to Christ and baptized, and the whole experience taught me just how hard it is to lead a church through renewal. The archaic and dysfunctional system of governance was a major reason why I resigned, knowing it would take more years to lead this church to renewal than I felt I had to give.

In my work with declined churches over the last few years, I have come to realize just how common the church council system of governance is . . . and how effective it is at keeping small, dysfunctional churches that way. From some historical research, I learned that the council form of governance was derived from a 19th century business and municipal governance model, in which all departments of the corporation or municipality were brought together periodically to report on their activities. It was applied to the local church as a way to enhance communication and decentralize power so that certain individuals, especially the clergy, would not accrue too much authority. Church councils are still common among smaller, congregationally governed churches such as Baptist or Congregational churches.

I believe this system works against revitalization for the following reasons:

1. The system is designed to limit the authority of the pastor. But a pastor *must* be given enough authority to function as the leader of change if the church is to be renewed.
2. It keeps the committee heads focused on their individual areas of interest, not on the common mission of the church.
3. It creates turf wars as each committee competes for its share of scarce resources, so leaders are not inclined to support new initiatives that they suspect will diminish those resources.
4. Church councils are certainly not biblical, nor rooted in Protestant theology.

5. They thrive on mistrust and suspicion of pastoral authority.
6. They create an unequal distribution of power so that those with little responsibility have the same authority as those who carry most of the responsibility.
7. They elevate the most insignificant matters in the church and waste the time of the church leaders in discussing them.
8. They are easily manipulated by aggressive personalities.
9. They provide a forum for every complaint, regardless of the nature of the complaint or the motivation of the complainer.

Even though, thanks to my predecessor, I did not have that to deal with a council in my first church, I still had to work with and within a very cumbersome structure. The Deacons and Trustees were the two leading boards, and they often clashed. The Deacons wanted to introduce new ministries, but if there was a cost, the Trustees would withhold approval. I spent my days running between the two committees trying to get them to work together. The Music Committee triangulated my work with the organist/choir director. I would tell him one thing, and they would tell him another. I recall him coming to me in exasperation wondering to whom he should answer. Furthermore, the bylaws stated that the pastor was an ex officio member of every committee and as such was expected to attend as many meetings as possible. My evenings were spent among committees where I had no opinion and no authority. At first, it was a good way to get to know the church members and the workings of the church. But it soon became clear that this system had to change if the church was to be revitalized. Too much of a pastor's time and energy, as well as that of the members, is spent in meetings. In a committee-system church, there is no space in members' lives for personal spiritual growth or "the works of service so the body of Christ may be built up" (Ephesians 4:12).

Early in my ministry, I was overwhelmed with the hospital and nursing home visits to scores of aging members. I cautiously approached my deacons, many of whom were also elderly, wondering if they could help. I was surprised when most of them enthusiastically said yes. I formed a visitation group within the deacons and named it the Kaleo Fellowship, using the New Testament word for "call." They liked the name as it meant their calling as deacons and also that they were calling on the aged and the sick. The Kaleo team knew most of the people they visited, they felt valued, and it helped me in this important work of caring for the flock. I continued to visit, but with Kaleo, more people were cared for by more people. It was a wonderful thing to see deacons in their eighties praying with people in nursing homes and hospitals. Kaleo Fellowship was our first small but successful effort in releasing the body of believers to serve Christ in works of ministry.

After several years of dealing with the byzantine committee system while also trying to lead the church back to vitality, we initiated the coordinating group that I described in Chapter 7. I did not realize it at the time, but this set the stage for our eventual transition to a system of elders.

THE ELDER SYSTEM

The coordinating group worked well for about a dozen years. It freed our leadership to start Bible studies within the church and outreach ministries to the community. As the church gradually grew, I felt we needed to formalize the coordinating group in order to help me lead the church. The pastor of a nearby Congregational church shared how his church had transitioned to an elder system. I immediately sensed that God was speaking to me and that, after years of awkward and redundant church governance, it was time to do something different. I realized that our coordinating group composed of senior leaders had in fact been functioning like an eldership. I also realized that the high level of trust within the coordinating group, and toward the group from the congregation, would make reorganizing the church structure easier.

In my study of the Scriptures, it was evident that both Old and New Testaments talk about elders. Tribal elders provided leadership for the community of God's people in ancient Israel. In the New Testament, elders were appointed in every church to provide leadership.

In addition, John Calvin taught that elders were one of the three major offices of the church, along with pastor-teacher and deacons. The Pilgrims, Puritans, and early New England Congregationalists all saw the role of elders as that of providing leadership for the local church along with the pastor and under the authority of the congregation and Christ. I wondered why Congregational churches of today rarely if ever had elders. As I read further into early American church history, I discovered that in the early 19th century, New England Congregational churches did away with the elder system because lifetime elders were usurping power from the local congregations and pastors. Congregational churches were in danger of becoming Presbyterian, with final authority shifting from the congregation to a body of elders. Because elders were appointed for life in those days, they often outlasted the pastor and accrued more power the longer they served. My church had been founded in the mid-19th century, after this shift away from elders had occurred, and so never had elders.

I came to realize that the whole notion of an elder structure flows out of the ancient family system of tribes. Virtually every small community and church has de facto elders. It is a very natural, organic way to provide leadership. Every community has people who by virtue of their age, life experience, and servant leadership have gained wisdom and the trust of others in that community. The tribal elder may be the oldest, universal form of human governance.

In my own church, I was able to trace the outline of an elder *function* through our church's history. It took various forms, such as an executive committee of deacons who, with the pastor, set the church's agenda. From its founding, there was always a single group of de facto "elders" who were looked to for leadership and guidance. It was only in the 20th century that the church shifted to a council system, which not only failed to give effective leadership but also became an obstacle to growth. Like most mainline churches, my church grew steadily up to the mid-20th century. Then, it plateaued and began a long, gradual decline. In my opinion, the loss of the "elder" function was one of the factors that contributed to its decline.

In my thirteenth year, as the church had grown and as I had won the trust of the congregation I floated the idea of moving from our committee system to an elder structure. We spent a year talking about it, studying relevant texts, preaching, praying, discussing, and interviewing church leaders in our area whose churches had already made the change. We sensed that God was leading us in this direction. We learned much from our study. As a result, we made what I feel were some very wise decisions about the shape our elder structure would take. Here is a summary of those decisions.

1. We would call the structure an elder board because that is what it is and that is the biblical term. Some churches may feel comfortable with another term.
2. The board, along with the pastor, would have overall supervision for the church, including oversight for all ministries and for the fiscal and physical assets. In effect, it combines the work of the deacons and trustees.
3. It would have six members, plus the pastor, making it small enough to operate efficiently.
4. Members would be elected to serve a three-year term and could not succeed themselves, except to fill an unfinished

term. There would be no lifetime elders, because biblically eldership is an office, not a spiritual gift. A spiritual gift is for a lifetime; an office is for a season.

5. The pastor would be an ex officio member of the board, meaning that he or she need not be elected but serves as a full voting member by right of the office of pastor.

6. The pastor would not chair the board. Knowing that pastors accrue more and more power the longer they serve, it was important to limit that power. (I did meet regularly with the chair to set the agenda.)

7. The board would operate in unanimity, not with a simple majority. This was probably the most important decision we made. We trusted that Christ, as head of the church, would not lead some members to one opinion and other members to a different opinion. The Body of Christ is not divided. When faced with a decision, the elders would pray and deliberate as long as was needed to reach unanimity. In the vast majority of decisions, full agreement was reached almost immediately. Over the years, however, there were a handful of important decisions that took us weeks to reach unanimous agreement. As a result of this unanimity provision, there have been no serious conflicts in this church for more than three decades—and this was a church with a history of conflict. When all that is required is a simple majority vote, there are always winners and losers. The winners feel justified and prideful, and the losers feel defeated and disconnected. That is often the beginning of factions and division. When the elders are in harmony, the harmony extends to the whole church body. The unity of the body must begin with the leaders, and unanimity provides for that.

8. The major role of the elders is to listen to the Head of the body, Jesus Christ (Colossians 1:18), discern what He is

saying, and then lead the church to obey. Discernment and wisdom are vital spiritual gifts for elders to have.

9. The elders submit to the will of the congregation through an annual, congregation-wide meeting, plus any other congregational meetings that may be needed for major decisions.

10. The pastor would choose his or her own staff, but the elders would be responsible for the actual hiring, compensation, and staff discipline or dismissal. This difficult issue of staff discipline is thus lifted from the pastor's shoulders. Only the senior pastor is called by the whole congregation and is liable to dismissal by a majority congregational vote. The rest of the staff can be terminated by a (unanimous) vote of the elders, which includes the pastor.

11. The elders, not the pastor, would be responsible for church discipline of members. This also removed the pastor from this potentially risky task.

12. The pastor is the only staff member who can be an elder. This was very important because it gave the pastor a trusted forum to discuss staff matters.

13. Only one member from a family could be an elder at any given time.

14. Future elders would be chosen by a nominating committee with the recommendation of the pastor and current elders. Qualifications for elders come from I Timothy 3 and Titus 1. These biblical descriptions focus on character, quality of family life, and skills in ministry leadership.

15. A mutually agreed-upon elder covenant binds the elders together in their functioning.

16. Both men and women can be elders since, in our tradition, women can also serve as pastors. In New Testament culture it made perfect sense to have only male elders, but there are no explicit biblical prohibition for women elders.

Women and men bring different gifts and temperaments to the task of leadership, and I believe both are needed.

17. Our reading of the New Testament led us to see elders primarily as leaders, not teachers. The pastor is the main teaching elder.

We made the initial transition from our trustee/deacon committee structure to elders simply by appointing three of our deacons and three of our trustees (chosen by their boards) to become the first elders. Two agreed to serve a 1-year term, two a 2-year term, and two a 3-year term. From then on, two new elders were nominated each year and then elected at the annual congregational meeting.

With the elders overseeing the whole ministry, the various committees became unnecessary, and instead ministry teams were created and reported periodically to the elders. The teams included children's ministry, worship, missions, and occasionally others as needs arose. For example, sometimes when a task was only for a season, such as a building project, an ad hoc team was formed. The elders vested these ministry teams with authority so that the members who were responsible for the work also had the authority to do the work. Also, the members did not need to be reappointed each year since their work was ongoing. However, they were confirmed each year at the annual meeting. The elders trusted these teams and gave them wide latitude to operate. A wonderful spirit of trust existed between the various ministry teams and the elders as long as prayer and unity were paramount.

As our church grew in size, the job of day-to-day governance shifted from the elders to the full- and part-time staff members. The role of elders became that of providing a protective covering for the ministry staff. They also set policy, exercised discipline, prepared the budget, and oversaw the hiring; and with the pastor and staff, they set the overall direction for the church. All this was with the support of the congregation. The leadership of our

161

renewed church could be summarized this way: "Staff led, elder guided, and congregation governed."

The decision to revamp our organizational structure around an elder-guided function was one of the most important decisions the church made in the 35 years of my tenure. It allowed us to discern the vision God was giving and to set the direction to fulfill it. It allowed us to respond quickly to major ministry opportunities, and it enabled us to enjoy decades of spiritual unity and harmony. Most important, it aligned the church with a biblical governance structure.

When a church has begun to be renewed and the trust level in the church is strong enough, it makes sense to realign the church's governance structure to a more biblical one. Do not be in a hurry. Take the time needed to prayerfully introduce and implement such changes. But know that renewal of church structure not only gives evidence of revitalization, it also enhances ongoing revitalization efforts.

13

The Renewal of Leadership

As a church begins to be renewed, the leadership of the church also starts to change. Some leaders step aside willingly, feeling that they have done their job guiding the church through difficult years of decline and bringing it to a new place. These leaders are self-aware; it is obvious to them that newer, younger leaders are needed. They are happy to hand off leadership to others who can bring new spiritual gifts and experiences. These former and often older leaders are the faithful and rare John-the-Baptist types who say, "I must decrease and he must increase." Such leaders are a blessing to a revitalization pastor. Often, they become trusted advisors who use their wisdom to continue to help the church in an unofficial, tribal elder capacity.

Then, in contrast, there are leaders who refuse to give up the power and control they have exercised over the years. Some of these men and women sincerely believe that they know what is best for the church. After all, they were here long before the current pastor and helped keep the ship afloat in turbulent waters. They are familiar with all the workings of the church and genuinely think that their leadership is essential for the life of the church. Other long-time leaders have motives for clinging to power that are not so benign. These individuals believe it is their duty to prevent the church from changing. These leaders see that the same loyal members keep being nominated to new terms on committees or, if there are term limits, rotated to other committees. Thus they become what author Thom Rainer refers to as the "cartel."

The cartel works against new pastors by denying them the leadership authority that they need to move the church forward. The longer the cartel stays in power, the more conflict there will be with the pastor, and the longer revitalization will take. The cartel keeps new members out of power, thwarting their desire to serve the church and making it more likely they will leave. New members will wait only so long for an opportunity to serve the church before they look elsewhere to use their gifts.

The cartel also keeps the church program-oriented rather than mission-oriented, leaving the same ministries in place long after they have ceased to be effective. No one ever questions the existence of the outmoded programs; they are simply refunded and restaffed annually.

In the process of church revitalization, a time comes when those who fully support the pastor's leadership begin to outnumber the cartel and their followers. As this tipping point nears, the cartel will fight harder to hang onto power. In Chapter 8, I related the story of reaching the tipping point in my 10th year of pastoral ministry. With the church on the verge of significant renewal, the cartel in my church fought their final and fatal battle. After that, the church was truly set free in wonderful ways to worship, to evangelize, to disciple, and to serve the community all in fulfillment of Christ's mission. I learned some important lessons about leadership during those years that I think are worth sharing.

LEADERSHIP LESSONS LEARNED

First, the need for gifted, faithful leaders is present in every church at all times. Jesus warned us that the workers would always be few (Matthew 9:37). So the leadership vacuum is not something you solve once and for all. I often think of New England Patriots head coach Bill Belichick's situation at the end of every season, and especially after a Super Bowl victory. After the enormous effort of assembling a championship team, the coach must start all over again next season. Veteran players exercise their free agency and move to other teams for higher salaries. They have their Super Bowl rings, and now they want a greater financial reward; and who can blame them. You will feel the same way when you see leaders that you have carefully and prayerfully recruited, discipled, trained, and deployed move on because of job relocations, or because another church has better programs for their children, or because family or personal schedules no longer allow them to serve. Then like the head coach you have to begin again. It can get very discouraging for any pastor but especially for the pastor engaged in a church revitalization. We have to just accept the fact that finding, recruiting, developing, and deploying leaders to build up the body IS the work of ministry (Ephesians 4), and not a distraction from ministry.

Second, understand and accept your starting point—that is, the condition of your church when you began your ministry—and be patient with the leaders you inherited. God in His sovereignty has allowed them to be there. Some of them have stayed with the church through very difficult times. Honor their faithfulness. Some are simply filling a slot for which they have no gifting. Some may actually be working against you and to the detriment of the church because of their lack of leadership gifts or their cranky personality. They sincerely but erroneously believe they are helping the church by resisting your authority.

In the first year of my first pastorate, a new chairman was elected to the diaconate. At the first meeting, he looked at me and announced in the presence of the whole board: "My job as chairman is to protect the church from you." I was stunned, but in my youth and inexperience I said nothing. He then went on to rehearse the history of the recent past, when the church split over the dictatorial leadership of the previous pastor. The younger families left, but before they did they forced his resignation. What was left in the church was a core of mostly older people, and this chairman was determined that I would not cause any further damage. Over the next year, I submitted to his leadership as he controlled every aspect of the deacons' work. I worked hard to maintain harmony on the board and in the church, but it was not easy working with this man. When that first year was over, I thanked God that now we might get a chairman who would share leadership with me. You can imagine how disappointed I was when he appointed himself chairman for a second year. I remember going home after that meeting and getting down on my knees and saying to the Lord, "I don't understand how I can work with this man for another year, but if that is what you want, I'll try my best."

That next year this man, who was my father's age, softened his approach to me. He insisted that we meet each month for lunch at a local restaurant to plan the meeting agendas. Over a two-martini lunch (him not me) that he paid for, we worked together. We actually became friends, and he shared with me the story of his difficult life and how years earlier, following a near fatal heart attack, he had given his life to Christ. His company eventually moved him out of state, and a few years later he died suddenly of a heart attack. I officiated at his funeral and was able to truthfully say that we had become good friends and that I knew he was with the Lord. I am forever thankful that I accepted the starting point and submitted to his authority out of obedience to Christ.

Third, there is no such thing as group leadership. A group can maintain the church for a while, sometimes a long while. But sooner or later you as pastor have to be given the right to fulfill your calling to be a shepherd and lead the sheep. Your leadership must always be with the willing support and consensus of the people. It can never be dictatorial. But you must lead your church. Even more, you must become comfortable with your role as leader and embrace it.

Fourth, wait for God's timing. I learned that God does faithfully raise up the leaders needed at any given time. Jesus reminded his disciples that the harvest will always be plentiful and the workers few, so they should "ask the Lord of the harvest . . . to send out workers into his harvest fields" (Matthew 9:37-38). I can recount numerous times when, seemingly out of the blue, God sent us the leaders we needed. Sometimes, someone who had been on the sidelines of the church would unexpectedly respond to God's call to serve. Other times, mature Christians moved to the area, and into our church, who had been evangelized, discipled, trained in leadership, and were willing and eager to serve. I recall one family who relocated temporarily to our town from Southern California and in their short time with us helped transform our children's ministry with their fresh approach to Sunday school and Vacation Bible School leadership. They brought a level of excellence to planning, programming, and training that continues to this day. A pastor needs to be faithful in praying to the Lord of the harvest to send those leaders that He is preparing. And then thankfully receive the gifts He sends.

Waiting for God's timing sounds almost trite, yet it is one of the hardest leadership lessons to learn. And if you are like me, it has to be relearned over and over. As caring shepherds, we see ministry needs and opportunities everywhere, and the urge to do something—anything—is strong. But as someone has wisely said, "The need does not constitute the call." If you see a need but don't see anyone called and ready to lead the response, then wait. Don't push anything in ministry that you aren't prepared to push forever. If you start it by offering to lead, you'll own it. Wait for God's timing and trust that, if it is His will, at just the right time He will call forth a leader to meet the need.

Fifth, offer training for your volunteer leaders. It is a mistake to assume that your leaders know what to do. A few leaders are born, but most are made. Write good job descriptions and let them know your expectations. Take the time to meet with your leaders to evaluate them, encourage them, pray with them, and help them see the Kingdom benefit of what they are doing. It is admittedly a challenge to carve out the time to spend with leaders, but in the long run, it will pay great dividends.

Sixth, understand, teach, and apply "gift theology." As your church begins to be renewed, you will move away from the old system of filling committees with anyone who volunteers or can be persuaded. Instead, choose and use leaders according to their spiritual gifts. Both the Old and New Testaments teach about gifting by the Holy Spirit for the work of ministry. In Exodus we see the example of the tabernacle craftsmen Bezalel, Oholiab, and others anointed by the Holy Spirit to build the tabernacle. In four extended passages in the New Testament (Romans 12, I Corinthians 12, Ephesians 4, and I Peter 4), the Apostles go into great detail regarding spiritual gifts. It is essential to develop your own biblical understanding of spiritual gifts and to appreciate how important the deployment of gifts is to the renewal and healthy functioning of the church. A pastor equipped with and guided by an understanding of gift theology will make better choices in leadership development. We know from the plain teaching of Scripture that it is through the discovery and application of spiritual gifts that the church functions and fulfills its mission. It is obvious that spiritual gifts are incredibly important given their prominence in the Scriptures, so let me say more about applying gift theology to the renewal of church leadership.

GIFT THEOLOGY

I believe that the whole understanding of spiritual gifts has often been hijacked by much recent and bad church theology. Teaching about spiritual gifts is frequently reduced to what can become a narcissistic quest for self-discovery. Many spiritual gift inventories have been produced, and yes some are good, (for example, *S.H.A.P.E.: Finding & Fulfilling Your Unique Purpose for Life*, from Saddleback Ministries, and *Network: The Right People, in the Right Places, for the Right Reasons, at the Right Time*, developed by Willow Creek Associates), and yes I have given my share of gift inventories. Spiritual gift assessment tools are useful to a point, but in many cases they put the cart before the horse. They get the Christian believer focused on himself or herself and not on the church body. Too often the result is that people fill notebooks with a thorough analysis of their gifts but rarely get around to actually using them.

I believe a better approach to the discovery and deployment of gifts is to first teach about them from the pulpit and in Bible studies. Then encourage the congregation to take some small first steps in doing something in the service of Christ. As the old saying goes, "You can't steer a parked car." Often it is in the process of serving that a Christian discovers his or her gifts. The simplest definition of a spiritual gift that I ever heard is that it is "how God uses you to build up the church"—that is, to fulfill His purposes. I believe that we discover whether we have a gift of teaching, for instance, when we actually teach and see people actually learn. Years ago, our church introduced a program for newcomers and new believers called "First Serve." It outlined many low-demand service opportunities on Sunday mornings or during the week. These gave newcomers and new believers a chance to test out spiritual gifts such as mercy, or hospitality, or serving, or administering. In this way members gained confidence and awareness of their gifts. We encouraged people to step out in faith, begin moving, and in that way discover their gifts and the direction God was leading them.

Over time, gift theology puts an end to the "musical chairs" approach to lay leadership in the church. Typically a church in decline deploys people by "filling the slots" with anyone who will serve, willingly or reluctantly. As in musical chairs, the same small pool of people keep serving by rotating positions, thus ensuring that no new ideas bubble up and nothing changes. No discussion or thought is given to whether these slots are actually needed or really accomplish anything. No discussion of spiritual gifts ever takes place, or whether those serving possess the right gifts for the job. In declined churches, spiritual gifting is rarely ever mentioned, and there is little understanding and application of spiritual gifts. If gifts are taught at all, it is probably from a "charismatic" standpoint with an emphasis on the dramatic gifts such as tongues speaking. In my experience this gift, though usually genuine and certainly biblical, is the least helpful for building up the Body. In fact, the Apostle Paul makes it clear that in tongues speaking the individual edifies himself and *not* the church.

Gift theology also challenges what I call the "talent show" approach that often characterizes declined churches, especially in worship leadership. Churches are families, and small churches are small, close-knit families. Every family member who wants to serve may serve, regardless of whether they are called or gifted to serve in a particular way. For example, if someone wants to preach, or sing, or play an instrument, they are allowed to simply because they want to or feel they have talent to do so. The result is sometimes quite literally a cacophony of noise. We all have seen young children playing a squeaky violin or plinking on a piano during Sunday worship because their parents wanted them to. While everyone smiles at the cuteness of the scene, there is no thought to spiritual gifts and how this helps people worship. On the other end of the age spectrum, we have all heard soloists who should no longer be singing. In this case the result is not smiles but a "lint-picking" moment—in other words, a situation so socially awkward that you can't make eye contact and so resort to picking dust off your lap. Again, no thought was given as to whether this person is called and gifted to lead people in sacred worship.

I inherited a talent show worship philosophy in my first church. Every year, we held three special Sunday services not on the liturgical calendar. One was Layman's Sunday, when the deacons were responsible for leading worship and preaching. Now sometimes this turned out well, but more often not so well. Usually, an individual with no training in biblical teaching would simply read some moralistic thoughts for the sermon. Later we were able to replace the "sermon" with a testimony of a deacon's personal spiritual journey, which often was very moving and encouraging. The second special service was Boy Scout Sunday, when the scout troop our church sponsored would conduct the worship service, with one of the Boy Scout leaders appointed to preach. While this was good public relations for the troop and helped the congregation learn more about scouting, it was clearly not gift theology in action. The third special Sunday was Masons Sunday. On this day, members of the church who belonged to the local Masonic Lodge would conduct the service and sometimes even preach the sermon. These Sundays always bothered me because I knew the broken hearts and shattered lives of many of my congregants. How many people came burdened, longing to hear a word from the Lord? And how many went away disappointed when sacred worship was led by those neither gifted nor called to lead. Over time as I preached about spiritual gifts and we spent time in small group Bible study, we gained an understanding of how God wanted to work to revitalize his church. All three of these services were eventually discontinued.

The talent show and musical chairs approaches to leadership deployment are how declined, demoralized churches operate. But God intends His church to operate differently. At some point, a replant pastor has to begin teaching, and a church must begin living out a biblical understanding of spiritual gifts.

As noted, a theology of spiritual gifts appears in both the Old and New Testaments. The biblical meaning of *gift* includes two ideas: first, the idea of gift as a talent, an innate ability; and second, the idea of gift as something given by someone else, namely the Holy Spirit. In English, we use the word *gift* in the same two ways. We say a talented person has a gift of music or athleticism, and we call a birthday or Christmas present a gift. A biblical understanding of gifts includes both of these meanings: a talent and a present. Many gift inventories lean more on the talent side, so the emphasis is on the individuals and their aptitudes. We need to balance that with the notion of a gift received from the Spirit and then given away to others so the church is built up. Then the focus is not on self but on the others for whom the gift is intended.

The Protestant Reformers understood spiritual gifts in this latter sense. The person ministering is given the gift by God, not to be possessed but to be delivered to the body of believers. So someone with a gift of teaching uses that gift to benefit his or her students. Someone with a gift of mercy uses that gift to benefit people in need or pain. And so on. God endows every believer with gifts, and like the UPS or FedEx delivery driver, the believer's job is to deliver the gift to those who need it. The gifts originate with God, or in our delivery analogy, the sender. They are intended for the benefit of the church, or the customer. They are delivered by the Christian who has received the gift, or the carrier. At the end of the day, the purpose of the sender is fulfilled: the customer has the package, the truck is empty, and the driver's job is done. The gift does not belong to the carrier, and it does not remain with him. He is simply the delivery vessel. He knows that he has done his job when the sender (God) is happy, the customer (the church) is blessed, and the truck and driver (the gifted person) is empty but fulfilled. Every preacher knows that empty but fulfilled feeling on Sunday afternoons, after faithfully using the gifts of preaching and teaching to build up the Body.

Given the importance of spiritual gifts, it is not surprising that the writers of Scripture devote so much attention to them. This is how Christ intends for his church to function properly. I wish I had spent more time early on teaching about spiritual gifts. I could have spent less time fussing with spiritual gift inventories and more time helping people sort through the trial-and-error process of discerning how God has used them to bless others, and then encouraging them to use those gifts to build up the church in servant leadership.

When pastors have spent time teaching about spiritual gifts, they can then confidently move away from the "filling the slots" or "talent show" approach to leadership. When needed, they can say, "I don't think that is your spiritual gift, but let me help you discover what your gift is." The renewal of church leadership is not about getting people to do what we want but about helping members discover and cultivate their gifting and their calling to fulfill God's will.

A BIG VISION ATTRACTS LEADERS

One reason why a church may not be attracting leaders is that there is nothing exciting or gripping about what it is doing. We all want our lives to count, to make a difference. We all, and especially we leaders, are attracted to a compelling vision and want to be part of it.

Just a couple of years into my first pastorate (in the late 1970s), a ministry colleague phoned me with a request. He worked for World Relief's refugee resettlement program and was calling about WR's urgent need for local churches to sponsor Southeast Asian refugees. Thousands had fled their homelands after the fall of South Vietnam and were being held in overcrowded camps. The U.S. government had agreed to take in a generous number of these families if citizen sponsors could be found. Would our church be a sponsor? I promised to bring his request to the deacons.

At the time, most of our deacons were elderly, and most of our meetings were spent discussing who would serve communion and who was in the hospital. I was amazed when they enthusiastically agreed to support a family, IF we could find someone to take leadership. They all felt it was the right thing to do, and many signed up to help, but none felt qualified to lead the charge.

Imagine my surprise the next Sunday morning. No sooner had I announced the need than a young couple new to the church stepped forward to volunteer. They gathered and organized helpers, and we soon welcomed a Cambodian family with two little children. Everyone on the sponsorship teams pitched in to meet the many needs—finding an interpreter, locating and furnishing an apartment, placing the family with appropriate agencies for benefits, getting the kids into preschools and the parents into jobs, even connecting them with a Cambodian church in the next town.

The young couple from our church who gave extraordinary leadership to the effort eventually got involved with that Cambodian church and helped evangelize a large displaced population. His name was George, but we dubbed him St. George, patron saint of refugees. Neither St. George nor any of his leadership team had been attracted or inspired by the routine business of our church. But this vision was from God, and it was compelling.

14

The Renewal of Staff

As a church undergoes revitalization and sees growth, the deployment of additional staff becomes necessary. Knowing when and whom to designate as staff is both exciting and challenging.

STAFFING FOR GROWTH

Volunteer or paid staff should be added to help move the church toward fulfilling the mission and vision that have been discerned. Here is the order of staff additions that I recommend. In my opinion, the second most important leadership position after the pastor is the worship/music leader. It is also the most difficult to get right, so take your time. (For more on this, see Chapter 11.) If the church is to have any hope of ministering to young families, then the third most important staff position is a director of children's ministry. Fourth, hire or secure an administrator who can keep all the moving parts in sync and serve as the day-to-day communicator and manager of staff and volunteers. This person frees you up to teach, shepherd, disciple, pray, and lead, after the fashion of the appointment of deacons in Acts 6. The fifth position is a small group coach and coordinator, as discipleship and training happen best in small group settings. This person can oversee outreach ministries like Alpha, Divorce Care, and other small-group-based ministries. In my opinion, a youth minister would come sixth unless you already have a large number of teens in the church. A better approach is to organize committed and skilled parents into a volunteer team to lead the youth ministry until it demands greater gifts of time and talent to lead.

Part-Time, Not Full-Time

Since most churches in renewal have very limited budgets, part-time is best. Sometimes churches make the mistake of hiring a full-time associate to wear a number of different hats. I say "mistake" because, first, it is very costly to hire a full-time person. A full-time staff position may involve relocation costs, housing costs, medical insurance, a retirement package, expense account, office space, and administrative support. Second, it is a mistake because people have strong areas and weak areas. It is rare to find someone able to minister equally in a variety of areas. Invariably associates play to their strengths and interests, which may be the same as the senior pastor's. To me, part-time specialists is the better way to go.

Pilots, Not Co-Pilots

At the risk of offending all of the associate pastors out there, I think the notion of an associate pastor is misguided. I speak from experience. I was once an associate pastor, and I hired four associate pastors over a period of 10 years. After the fourth, I realized why the whole idea is flawed. (I am a slow learner.)

Associate pastors are usually hired as a second generalist (after the pastor, who needs to be a generalist as well). They are typically hired to do those pastoral tasks that the senior pastor does not like to do or is not gifted for, such as visitation or administration. The problem is, usually the associate does not like to do those things either.

Within six months of hiring our fourth associate, I knew we had made a mistake, but it was six years before we could move him on to a secular career, for which he was better suited. He was a good and godly person but a classic "silo-er." For instance, he would take assignments but never give an accurate report of progress, so I never knew what he was doing. He appeared to be working hard, but nothing ever got done. Repeated attempts to hold him accountable failed because he was a master of subterfuge. It was an easy and comfortable job for him, but he was contributing little to the mission of the church while consuming scarce resources. Along the way, he managed to gather around him a small but loyal following. So when I thought about trying to dismiss him, I realized we would probably pay a big price. I continued to try to work with him long after we should have let him go.

He had previously been a pastor of a very small church. They gave him a good reference, but in hindsight I realize it was to move him on because of his similar ineffectiveness there. A more thorough background search would have revealed this. Again, my mistake. We did finally succeed in letting him go, with a generous severance package including training in a field outside pastoral ministry. At this time, I learned a very important lesson from a commercial airline pilot. After observing everything, this pilot, a member of my congregation, told me that an associate pastor was like a co-pilot, except that in the airlines, co-pilots never exist. Airlines only hire pilots, who serve as co-pilots until they are ready to fly on their own. He suggested that there really is no such thing as associate pastors, either. They are pastors who are not yet ready to fly solo. He pointed out that the associate pastor in question had obviously failed as a "pilot" when he had served as a pastor, so he wondered why we had hired him in the first place. It was an epiphany for me. I realized that our first three associates had been pilots: they were smart, motivated, and gifted but just lacked the experience of pastoring. We gave them that, and after about 18 months on the job, each was restless and ambitious to fly solo. I got to recognize that faraway look in their eyes of wanting their own church pastorate. They were soon pastoring on their own and many years later are still having successful ministries. They touched a lot of lives for the short time we had them, and we helped prepare them to pastor on their own.

From then on, if we were going to hire associate pastors, they would be pilots, and we would help prepare them for pastoral leadership elsewhere in the Kingdom. What we would *not* do is hire an associate who either did not want to be a pastor or was not gifted to be one. After the costly learning experience with that associate, we never hired another generalist staff person, only specialists.

BUILDING YOUR STAFF TEAM

"Hire" Volunteers

One generalist pastor is enough. In a small church with very limited funds, volunteers can be given the status of part-time staff. Rather than adding them to the payroll, they can be rewarded with perks such as a title, office space, an expense account, and tuition reimbursement for courses, conferences, and degrees. If you decide to hire, a good rule of thumb is to look for people who are FAT: faithful, available, and teachable. Use the 70/30 rule: if they can do a job 70 percent as well as you can, give them the job, and help them grow the rest of the way. Train your volunteer staff. Do not assume they know how to do what you are asking. Create job descriptions with them and retrain as needed. I think one of the reasons for the extraordinary success of Alpha is that there are clear job descriptions for the various volunteer roles, and there is training and retraining for everyone, every time the course is offered. I served with our Alpha teams for nearly 20 years, and for every new session, I attended mandatory training sessions along with all of the other leaders.

Given the many competing demands of pastoral ministry, we seldom take the time to adequately train our staff. We simply throw them into a situation with a sink or swim attitude. No wonder the turnover of staff is so high. Look for seminars, conferences, or training opportunities to send your paid or volunteer staff to. Cover their expense and celebrate their completion of courses. Above all, pray for God to raise up the servant leaders that the church needs.

Hire from Within

The best people are often those from your own congregation, volunteers who have done an excellent job serving in some capacity and now are needed in a greater capacity. These people are proven, they have sticking power through their loyalty to the church, and they have earned the trust of the congregation. The time to move from volunteer to paid staff is when their workload exceeds what can be expected from a volunteer. If you hire the right people, they can be a blessing to the church for a long time. On the negative side if you hire the wrong people, it is difficult to remove them because of their relationship to the congregation.

Be Involved in Hiring

Do not abdicate your leadership as pastor and leave it to committees or elders to hire staff without your involvement. The hiring process should involve two votes, the elders' and the pastor's. If the pastor is not fully comfortable with the elders' choice, do not hire the person. Conversely, if the elders are not fully on board, you would be unwise to go against their opinion. Also, have your elders or leadership board, not the congregation, do the actual hiring. It is too cumbersome to have a congregational vote to hire or fire any staff other than the senior pastor.

Build Staff Cohesion

Have weekly staff meetings to pray, encourage, and remind everyone of the mission. Be their biggest cheerleader, praising them from the pulpit, telling the congregation what they do since their work may not be visible. Invite them to take part in the worship so they gain authority. Never throw them under the bus! Discipline privately, and protect staff from church bullies. Let them know you have their backs. Plan staff retreats and fun events. Remember, the community you seek to build in the church starts with your relationship to the people who are leading with you. If you are in true Christian community with them, it will trickle down to the congregation. As goes the leadership staff, so goes the whole church.

Inherited Staff

If you inherit staff, make every effort to work with them; they were here before you. Try to build a bond of trust with them, sharing your hopes for your ministry. Do not be surprised if they are resistant to your leadership and any changes you introduce. Like the congregation, they too have found their homeostasis and may see you as a threat to it. If possible, coach them in the expectations you have for them. If they are not skilled enough for the job, you may simply need to raise the level of expectation and see if they can rise to it. You may also need to be patient, accept what they can give, and trust God for the future. Remember that they are part of the family of God in your church, so handle with genuine care.

Unfortunately, insubordination on the part of an inherited staff person is very common in church revitalizations. If this is the case, after a sincere effort to work with them, you may have to bring in your leadership to resolve the problem. There is no room in the Body of Christ for insubordination, and this could be a deal breaker for your ministry if it is not resolved. Over time if you are prayerful, patient, and not overly anxious, these problems usually resolve. On the other hand, trying to remove a paid staff member for incompetence or insubordination can be very tricky. Many a new pastor has had to resign because he or she misjudged just how much power a secretary or music director had.

No Nepotism

Do not hire your family members. In church revitalizations, a pastor's spouse or children may be among the most skilled leaders available. And to be sure, the need for extra income is compelling. But no matter how tempting it is to hire family member, it is rarely a good idea. The most obvious reason is that it creates a triangle for the church: the congregation will not be able to criticize the family member for fear of damaging their relationship with the pastor. Everyone who receives a salary needs to be accountable and approachable. When this is not the case, it fosters resentment on the part of those paying the salary. In extreme cases, you will be forced to defend your spouse or son or daughter to the congregation, and that is never a good situation. The family member may not be effective, but a church cannot fire a member of the pastor's family without firing the pastor. A better alternative is to have your talented family member volunteer their gifts. This strategy puts them above most criticism and sets an example for others. They can also quickly and easily step down if necessary.

Also, you do not want your marriage and family life totally bound up in the affairs of the church, which may happen if you and your spouse are both on staff. Every clergy family needs a life outside the church. Our identity is ultimately in Christ and not in the church.

During this productive season in the life of a church, revitalization pastors are faced with the limitations of their time, energy, and gifting. The patient catalyst longs to see God raise up other gifted leaders to help bring about the beautiful diversity of the Body of Christ and rejoices when He does.

15

The Renewal of Membership

A healthy church always functions with two sets of expectations: LOW expectations of anyone who wants to attend and worship, and HIGH expectations for those who wish to become members or serve as leaders. The walk-in "foyer" of the church should be wide open and inviting, whereas access to the "living room" and "kitchen"—where intimacy is shared and big decisions are made—should be more limited and demanding. During this season in the revitalization process, these dual expectations should become reality. The result is a renewal of church membership and church membership qualifications.

WHO CAN JOIN YOUR CHURCH?

Unfortunately, as churches decline, so do their membership expectations. Declining churches are typically desperate for "new blood" to stanch the flow of those leaving the church through death, inactivity due to age or illness, or relocation, such as to assisted living facilities or faraway family. As a result, the standards for membership are dismally low.

In the church I pastored briefly in retirement, anyone wishing to become a member just had to sign the guest book at the back of the sanctuary! The following week, they were received into membership with full voting rights. Nor was anyone ever removed from membership rolls. This permissive practice had several unfortunate consequences. First, because there were no standards or expectations for members, some very troubled and difficult people gained positions of leadership. Second, there was a large inactive membership who rarely attended worship but could be mustered to attend congregational meetings when a group wished to oppose the pastor.

With a little detective work, I discovered that the bylaws actually required candidates for membership to present a written "statement of faith" confirming their commitment to Jesus Christ and to promise to worship faithfully, to support the church financially, and to walk in Christian love with the other members. Previous pastors, in their desperation for new members, had neglected to follow the bylaws, and no one objected. In my short tenure, I began to raise the bar. We would follow our own rules. I instituted a simple one-session membership "class" in which prospective members (with some coaching) wrote personal testimonies and then presented them to the board of deacons. During the session, I shared the basic gospel message and invited them to affirm their agreement. Then, we made much of the ceremony of publicly inducting individuals into membership during a worship service.

Had I stayed longer, my plan was to gradually expand the membership preparation to include a discipleship process. In the meantime, I simply "grandfathered" all of the existing members, some of whom were probably not even Christian believers. It seemed too disruptive to the congregation to back up and suddenly ask more of them than they had committed to under the lax membership guidelines. I would have to trust Christ to know His true sheep, and not try to root them out myself.

Not all your members will want to stay, grandfathered or not. An unexpected result of a church revitalization is the departure of church members who for whatever reason are unable to support the vision and direction of the church under the pastor's leadership. Sometimes this happens early in ministry, as members realize they are not on the same page with the theology, style, or vision that is unfolding. More often, it happens later when those members who have resisted a pastor's leadership realize they are now outnumbered and their ability to influence events has waned. Pastors sometimes call this "addition by subtraction."

Mike McKinley, in his book *Church Planting Is for Wimps*, stresses the importance of having sound documents such as a statement of faith or membership expectations. The latter was historically written as a membership covenant. Such a covenant may be the only authority church leaders in non-hierarchical churches have. Where there is no bishop or presbytery or district superintendent to exercise church discipline, a covenant can accomplish this. Congregationally governed churches, such as Baptist and Congregational, were almost always founded with a membership covenant that clearly (and often eloquently) stated what new members agreed to uphold upon joining. When a member acts in a way that is harmful to the church body, leaders can hold them accountable for their own words, pledged publicly and before God when they joined the church. If your church does not have a membership covenant that explicitly states the beliefs and behaviors that you expect of members, then seriously consider adopting one.

THE MYTH OF SHEEP STEALING

When your church has begun to experience renewal, there will be some transfer growth as people in other declined churches see the evidence of new life and switch their allegiance. This transfer growth is often regarded as a negative phenomenon and condemned as "church hopping" or "sheep stealing." In an ideal world, all church growth would be conversion growth, people won to Christ out of the world, but transfer growth is a constant reality. People are continuously moving from one church to another for many reasons. The whole notion of sheep stealing is a fallacy. Pastors waste their time worrying about it and discussing it at their clergy gatherings.

Conventional church etiquette dictated that a pastor should try to guide newly arrived sheep back to their home pen. For several reasons this is futile. First, people are not sheep. We make our choices carefully and generally act in the best interest of our families and ourselves. Second, the process of leaving one church to go to another is often a long and deliberate process, not an impulsive move. It typically starts with some issue with the current church and a waiting period to see if the issue is resolved, during which time the person may meet with the pastor. Then, there is a gradual withdrawal from church activities, attendance, and last of all financial support. By the time a member of another church ends up in your pews, they have already "paid the freight." They have gone through this long process of separation from friends and even family, and from what is familiar. They have grieved all of the losses they have experienced. They have spent weeks or months in a state of limbo, separated from their former church family, but not yet part of a new one. When finally they settle in your church, they have already borne all of those costs, so to tell them they should go back to their old church is like turning away desperate swimmers as they try to climb onboard your lifeboat. Do not push them away. Instead, meet with them and try to ascertain why they left and what they hope your ministry will offer them. Tell them to take their time to be sure they are making a good choice. To call this process "sheep stealing" denies the difficult choice involved and impugns the ethics of the pastor whose church then receives these refugees.

When you are on the losing end of this situation, it is a major disappointment in a small church. And it hurts each time it happens. However, it makes little sense to persuade people otherwise once they have decided to leave your church. Instead, if possible, meet with them in an exit interview and try to learn what you can from their leaving. (Realistically, they will rarely tell you their true reasons.) Then send them off with your genuine blessing and grieve their loss.

This is where revitalization ministry is hard, and we must depend on Christ to build His church. I learned this lesson early in my ministry.

Within my first two years at the church, we experienced some modest transfer growth as we were the only evangelical church in a town of 30,000. Then, a colleague took another church in town. He was a gifted preacher and leader. He hosted a Christian television program on a major network in a major TV market. Almost overnight, I began to lose people to his church. I remember feeling discouraged and wondered why God had brought me to this town just to lose my congregation to another church. I tried to stay confident that God had called me there and would build His church through me. It was a struggle, but I remained faithful to that call, resigning myself to the fact that it was not going to be an easy ministry. Over the next few years, our church grew very slowly, but mostly through evangelism, and my colleague's church grew rapidly both by evangelism and transfer growth. I had to fight the feelings of envy as he reported the growth of his ministry. We became good friends, and I accepted the fact that my work would rest in the shadow of his ministry. Then suddenly, my colleague resigned when it was revealed that he had been sexually involved with a woman in his church. He left his wife, and the ministry, never to return to either. His church then took a hard left turn theologically, back to its liberal roots. Scores of those who had left our church came back, and others whom he had led to Christ also began attending and eventually joined. In time, many of them developed into the leadership of our church.

To this day, that other church has continued on a theologically liberal track and is in decline, and our church, now under my successor's leadership, continues to be blessed by many strong leaders who arrived in that wave. From this experience, I was reminded that my call was not a mistake. Only God can see around the corners in life, and while the loss of this brother to the ministry and his family was not God's will, God knew it was going to happen. Our little church was to be His witness in that community after all. Now decades later my former church is one of the healthiest churches in New England and one of the strongest witnesses to Christ in a large metropolitan area. All this to say, do not believe the myth of sheep stealing, learn what you can from those who leave, welcome those who arrive, and trust the results to the One who has promised to build His Church.

As our society increasingly becomes a culture of non-joiners, strong, clear membership expectations are vital to knowing who the sheep are.

16

The Renewal of Stewardship

Revitalization must be accompanied by the renewal of the stewardship of resources. Ideally, God's people would marshal their financial resources in a faithful and biblical way to enable the healthy functioning of the church. It is very likely that even in a declining church, somewhere in its history or founding, a small group of people paid an enormous price to call a pastor, organize a church, and build a building. What a legacy of hope and heroic sacrifice. Over time, though, that legacy of hope and sacrifice has been forgotten and replaced with a spirit of fear and a hoarding mentality.

Declining churches are risk averse. They fear the day when they will run out of money and be unable to pay a pastor's salary and keep the doors open. Often the membership consists largely of seniors who are getting by on a fixed income, and the question for them personally and for their church is "Will our money last?" It is not uncommon for declining churches to hoard large amounts of money in savings accounts or conservative stock funds, guarding against the day when the well runs dry. Overseed has worked with many churches in New England with small aging congregations and large endowments, including one church with an elderly flock of 40 people and $20 million in investments. Sadly, the hoarding mentality that infects these congregations prevents them from spending their savings on the pastoral leadership and ministry ventures that might lead them back to health. Of course, for every one church with a large bank account, there are hundreds that function month to month, spending only what they take in. In both cases, it is a spirit of fear and scarcity that haunts these churches.

FEARFUL STEWARDSHIP: SELLING THINGS AND RENTING SPACE

We know that biblically speaking the opposite of faith is not unbelief but fear. The opposite of faith is ultimately a fear that God will not deliver on his promises. This fear is as old as humanity and is the primal sin in the Garden of Eden. Adam and Eve were not simply rebellious, they were fearful that God would not provide them what they believed they needed, and so they grabbed it for themselves. It is this primal fear of want that grips declining churches. Somewhere along the line, they stopped believing in a God of provision and took it upon themselves to provide for all their needs. The results are twofold: (1) they may look to the world to provide, rather than God; and (2) they may give up sacred ministry space in favor of rental income.

In the first place, the focus becomes making money by selling things to the world rather than asking the congregation to give sacrificially out of God's provision. Churches begin to function like restaurants, selling meals to the community, or like craft shops and thrift stores, hawking their wares. Now, there is nothing wrong with church suppers or church fairs. In fact, they can be appropriate forms of outreach by aging congregations to the local community if the purpose is to serve the poor or to earn money to give to local charities. How wonderful it is when a church offers suppers as a way to gather the congregation together or to serve the homeless. But when a church sells meals to support itself, it is asking the world to pay for the church, and it is never the world's responsibility to pay for God's work. The same is true when the church holds rummage sales or craft fairs. The church is not only asking the world to pay for ministry but also competing with local businesses that market these same items. Often a small, declining church is so locked into these activities that it would be cruel for a pastor to take them away. For older people living on a fixed income, church suppers and fairs are a way for them to convert their time into money to support the church. A better approach would be to redirect the funds raised to support local mission opportunities. So that when the community buys the meals they know they are supporting a local charity.

In the second scenario, a declining church may seek to survive financially by renting its church property. Rental space is at a premium in most cities and towns, especially in centrally located churches, so the pressure to rent space is strong. The problem of course becomes the church's loss of access to that rented space. The choice is then between using the building to make money or using it to minister to the community. Sometimes a church can do both if, for example, the space is rented for childcare or a senior center. In most instances, however, renting the church property will complicate the core mission of making disciples.

The example of Jesus overturning the moneychangers' tables in the Temple is illustrative, but not for the reason we might expect. Jesus was not against what the moneychangers or the animal sellers were doing. Both were providing a necessary service for Jewish pilgrims compelled to travel to the Temple for sacred holy days. By law, they had to pay a Temple tax and offer animal sacrifices. The tax could not be paid in the many foreign currencies, nor could pilgrims travel conveniently with animals. These Temple merchants were providing an essential service, even if they were probably overcharging for it. The problem was not so much what they were doing as where they were doing it. The only room available in the Temple complex for this activity was the large outer Court of the Gentiles. It was here that non-Jewish God-fearers and seekers from all over the world could approach the very presence of God, but not if the space was filled up with the merchants. The clue to understanding the passage in this way is found in Mark's Gospel (Mark 11:17), where Jesus quotes the Prophet Isaiah (Isaiah 56:7), "'My house shall be called a house of prayer for all nations.' But you have made it 'den of robbers.'" The problem was that all the space in the Temple where "all nations" could come close to God was filled up with the merchants and their tables. There was simply no room for seekers after God. The same happens when a church surrenders its physical space to the merchants of its community; space for ministry is lost.

If a church is in this situation, it can gradually reclaim the space as lease agreements expire and a congregation assumes responsibility for supporting the ministry. It often takes time and a patient approach, but eventually a renewing church can reclaim its space for the Lord's work in the world. The church I served for most of my ministry was located in a vibrant downtown area where there was never enough commercial parking or office space. We were constantly approached by business owners wanting to rent parking or meeting space. We eventually adopted a policy of not renting, but instead offering our space free on special occasions to the town and local merchants if it did not interfere with our use. This policy meant we turned down some lucrative offers such as using our 90-foot tower to house cell phone antennas. The antennas would have been invisible and would have generated about $60,000 annually for the church, but neighbors voiced concerns (now scientifically unproven) of radiation emitted from the antennas. Installing the devices would have pitted the church against our neighbors, and that was not the witness to Christ we wanted. Further, it would have gone against our stewardship

191

practice. I was so proud of our elders who made the decision to turn down a substantial source of income, not hesitating at all to do what we believed was right.

Moreover, the policy of offering our space free to local businesses for special events allowed us to gain favor with local merchants. One Christmas is memorable. Each holiday season, downtown merchants held many festive events, among them a popular family Breakfast with Santa. One year, due to a new regulation, the town government was obligated to charge the merchants a substantial fee to rent a local auditorium to house the breakfast. I learned about their dilemma from the merchants association, of which I was a member. I checked with our leadership, and we agreed to offer them our beautiful fellowship space for the breakfast without cost. So on the first Saturday of December that year, hundreds of young families came into our fellowship space (much better space, by the way, than what the town offered) to have breakfast and a picture taken with Santa. The local newspaper ran this headline: "How the Town Grinch Tried to Steal Christmas and How The Church Saved It." The local merchants have sung our praises ever since as we continued to host Breakfast with Santa and other community events.

Some young families, having come through the door for a "neutral" event, began attending our church. Again, I put this in the category of what was said about the Jerusalem church in its early days when they "enjoyed the favor of all of the people." One of the wonderful resources that earlier generations sacrificed to provide is physical space in strategic locations. How good it is when a church uses its space to glorify God and bless the community rather than renting it to tax the community. This policy helps a church gain a hearing for Christ.

HEALTHY STEWARDSHIP: CONFIDENTIALITY

In small, declining churches there are no secrets. Everyone knows everybody's business. Each person's financial contribution is known by all, including the pastor. You know who gives the largest amounts and who gives little or nothing. When this is the case, though, it is hard to think of everyone equally. You will invariably treat the generous givers with deference and be disappointed with those who seem stingy. The problem of course is that you never know the real value of what people give. The generous giver may be able to do so much more, and the small giver may be sacrificing to give that amount. So the small giver is growing in discipleship and the large giver is not. Christian formation is the real goal of stewardship.

One of the most liberating moments for me came when, early on, I decided to stop looking at what my members gave. I recall seeing the weekly offering check from one of my leaders and being shocked at how small the amount was. I had just assumed that since that person exercised a lot of authority, he was also very generous. I was disappointed in him and found myself judging him. I knew that was wrong, so I decided to avoid knowing what each person gave. I asked the treasurer and the counters to institute a strict policy of confidentiality. I began teaching that everyone's giving was between them and God and that neither I nor anyone else knew what anyone gave.

Establishing full confidentiality in stewardship is wise. You then treat everyone the same. You also obey Jesus's commands in the Sermon on the Mount about not letting "your left hand know what your right hand is doing" and "giving in secret so that the Father who sees in secret will reward you." In this way, you refuse to assume the role of the Holy Spirit in motivating your people to give. You do this by letting the congregation know that their giving is between them and God and that a policy of confidentiality is in place to ensure this. You can truthfully say that neither you nor the leadership knows what anyone gives. Usually, only the collecting and counting team will know, and they are charged with keeping confidences. I believe it is impossible to be impartial when preaching about money if you know who is giving what. You will invariably aim your message toward those you think need to hear it, trying to motivate them to give more. Instead, we can trust that God will move people as the Word is taught.

When you observe a rule of confidentiality, you can preach about money with boldness because you truthfully have no idea who gives what. It sets you free from trying to motivate your people yourself. You are removed from the equation. If anyone feels convicted, it is from the Holy Spirit, not you. You teach stewardship primarily as a path to spiritual growth and secondarily as the means to support the mission of the church. And the Holy Spirit becomes your ally in the discipleship of giving.

The rule of confidentiality helped me teach the linkage between giving and spiritual growth. Each year at budget time, I could honestly say that the process was not about funding a budget but about being obedient to Christ. God would use our obedience to meet the church's financial needs. I used to remind our sometimes-worried leaders that God always pays for what He orders. My wife and I practiced tithing as a minimum, often giving more than 10 percent, especially when gifts to Christian organizations outside the church were added in. I also taught tithing from the pulpit, but I stressed *sacrificial giving* and urged people to give as the Lord guided. One Sunday, a member of the congregation, a self-employed house painter and new Christian, asked if he could "fithe." I thought he had mispronounced tithe, so I asked him what he meant. He explained, "Well, if 10% is a tithe, wouldn't 5% be a fithe?" Thus a new term was coined in our church, and I encouraged new believers to start with a fithe and work their way to the tithe. There was a great sense of grace on everyone's part and a joy in giving. And we always met the budget.

It was not long after the switch to this grace-based stewardship that we were able to detach the church's budget from the anticipated offering income. For years, the annual budget was driven by how much money the leaders expected would be received that year. The annual meeting and the budget approval always followed the annual stewardship drive. The first question at the annual meeting was always, "Are there enough pledges to meet the budget?" If the answer was yes, the budget was approved. If the answer was no, the budget was reduced to the level of the anticipated giving. Then one year, after we had begun trusting God with the stewardship, no one asked the question. The budget, which was based on what we believed God wanted us to do, was simply approved by the congregation without caring about how much was pledged. That was a great moment in the stewardship life of the church, and we never looked back.

These two practices of (1) making giving a confidential matter between the giver and God and (2) making tithing our personal minimum of giving did more for me than anything else in leading our church forward in stewardship.

OTHER SIGNS OF HEALTHY STEWARDSHIP

Freedom

Freedom replaces fear because the expectation is that God will provide for his church. There is a freedom to teach and talk about money. In a declining church money is a forbidden topic, although everyone knows who gives what. In a declining church the pastor is told not to preach about money, that people don't want to hear it. Yet the same church will demand that the pastor make Sunday announcements about the small amount that a church supper netted! As a church comes alive in Christ, there is a greater confidence that God has indeed been providing for the needs, and there is a joy in speaking about the congregation's role as the means of that provision. The pastor is encouraged that when he or she teaches biblical principles like tithing and sacrificial giving, people will actually do it. The testimonies of members who have seen God's hand of blessing as they have taken tithing seriously becomes a mark of their growing discipleship.

Generosity

In a healthy church, generosity replaces the hoarding mentality of limited supply. There is no need to build up an endowment; a small rainy day fund is enough so that capital campaigns are not needed for every unexpected expense. Also, the leadership gets a realistic idea of what it costs to support a pastor. There is no bullying the pastor as in the story of the deacon who prayed, "Lord, you keep our pastor humble, and we'll keep him poor." In a generous church, the pastor is enabled to live at the level of the average family in his or her community. The pastor develops a more healthy relationship with money as he or she also takes tithing and sacrificial giving seriously. Then he can truthfully say that he does not ask his congregation to do anything he is not willing to do.

Space and Time

Buildings are tools, not temples. Tools get dull and wear out; they need to be refurbished or even replaced. The church building, though it may be precious to many, is not sacred. The only sacred temples are the lives and bodies of believers individually and corporately. And the church, the *ecclesia*, is always people, literally the "ones called apart for Christ," not the building. The early Puritans had it right when they called their building the "meeting house," not the church. The rationale for spending money to maintain and improve the building is so that this tool might aid and not impede the work of the church so that God might be glorified. A theology of space answers those who see the building as a museum piece that cannot be tampered with. It also answers the modern-day Gnostics who do not believe the physical building matters at all and would rather see the money spent on missions.

196

They deny their own physicality and choose to believe that smelly restrooms and unsafe children's spaces will not hinder the work of Christ.

100-Year Vision

It's important for replant pastors, or any pastor for that matter, to realize they are part of a 100-year vision, that the church under their leadership is making decisions that will impact the future, four or five generations ahead. It is easy to see how decisions made in the past 100 years about the building, location, denominational ties, theology, or ministry direction have led a church to where it is today. If in God's wisdom, our Lord does not return in this century, then we will be impacting the church 100 years from now. Pastors need to think in that extended time frame.

Decisions and sacrifices we make today will either bless or burden unborn Christ followers in the 22nd century. Very few human institutions need to have that perspective. Not to be too dramatic, but future generations will either "rise up and call us blessed," or ask, "What were they thinking back then?" Corporate Christian stewardship includes a holy understanding of the resources of money, time, and space.

17

Why Am I Restless?

There comes a time in many marriages when a couple's life's work together is largely done. The long season of rearing children and launching them out into the world is finished; the arduous labor of building careers is completed; now a couple can enjoy the fruit of all of their labor. This stage in a marriage is often a defining moment. The partners either discover another and deeper reason for being together than just raising children and building careers, or they realize they have not succeeded in building a more lasting foundation and go their separate ways.

I have known too many couples who made it nearly to the finish line of their life's marathon and decided to call it quits. They will not enjoy the fruit of all of their labor together, after all. While we never know all the reasons and therefore cannot judge, to me it is still sad. One wonders what it would have taken to reinvent the

199

marriage. Could they have discovered a new and deeper purpose for being together and, as a result, been a blessing to future generations. On the other hand, couples can and do successfully navigate the uncertain waters of reinvention. They often celebrate the past and symbolize their commitment to what lies ahead with a ceremony to renew their wedding vows.

In a way, the same "fork in the road" is true in the pastorate, once a pastor and congregation have reached a place of real renewal. (Of course, in one sense the process is never entirely complete.) At this point of revitalization, a church and pastor need to reinvent their relationship or, like some couples, they will sense the marriage is over. Tragically, they will most likely part just at the point when the potential for further health and growth is greatest. The final section of this book deals with this season when pastors either depart or find new and compelling reasons to stay— through reinvention.

This season is often characterized by feelings of confusion that the pastor's role in the church is changing. During the process of revitalization, a church undergoes many changes in its culture. It is not just the congregation that feels out of sorts with these changes; often the pastor does as well. As a pastoral size congregation grows, it becomes what author Kevin E. Martin calls a transitional church. In other words, it enters an awkward phase in which it is no longer a pastoral size church in which everyone can relate to the pastor, but it is not yet a program size church in which people are connected to the church via ministries and the staff who lead them. Frankly, the transitional church is extremely tough, maybe the toughest, to pastor.

Having lived through all of the stresses of the transitional church myself, I find Martin's description of transitional churches very accurate. He delineates four characteristics that make them especially difficult:

- Transitional churches are highly stressful for pastors because of the gap between what they were and what they are becoming. They were comfortable as a pastoral size church, when the congregation and pastor related to one another. As they grow, the pastor must spend more and more time caring for leaders and less time with the congregation. Some members leave because they feel the pastor no longer has time for them. They also complain that they no longer know everyone because so many new people have joined. Many pastors struggle to accept the fact that they can no longer have the kind of relationship with everyone the way they used to.

- The transitional church has a constant shortage of leaders. It takes skilled and dedicated leaders to give direction to the programs that will eventually enable many people to feel connected to the church. Finding, training, and supporting those leaders are difficult tasks. Consequently, the few solid leaders, including the pastor, must wear many hats. And this often leads to burnout.

- Transitional churches also have a shortage of other resources, such as space, funds, and effective programs. They are like an army that is constantly advancing beyond the reach of its supply lines. This is extremely frustrating for pastors, who see opportunities for ministries all around but realize they cannot meet them.

- Finally, the transitional church experiences conflict between those who want it to stay small and those who want it to grow. Those who want it to remain a pastoral size church are suspicious of the newer people who have taken up leadership and want to change things. The new people are impatient with long-time members whom they see as resisting the pastor's and the Lord's leadership.

While this is all evidence that God is blessing the church and that it is coming more in line with the biblical model of the church (Ephesians 4), it is still an awkward season for everyone. The stress of this transitional season may become so acute that, as pastor, you may conclude that your church is outgrowing your gifting. You may feel you have become a victim of your own success. You may begin to doubt your call and wonder why God brought you this far, only to now abandon you. It is at this time, when you are on the verge of a new season of blessing, that the temptation to leave is often the strongest. In both marriages and ministry, reinvention is better.

My first suggestion for weathering this season of uncertainty is to find a coach. This is a time to get help from someone with the wisdom and experience to guide you in this wilderness of unfamiliarity. In the six-state New England region, Overseed is committed to recruiting, training, and supporting coaches who will mentor replant pastors.

ERR ON THE SIDE OF REMAINING

Fortunately, Scripture gives us clear guidance in this season of discernment. For me, the Apostle Paul's counsel in I Corinthians 7 was most helpful. We know a lot about the 1st century city of Corinth and the church that the apostle planted there. We know for instance that it was a large, prosperous, transient city with a diverse population of Jews, Greeks, slaves, and freemen. There were numerous cults and mystery religions. The dominant pagan deity was Aphrodite; the temple prostitution surrounding Aphrodite-worship helped foster a promiscuous culture. It was into this mix that Paul brought the gospel of Christ with its liberating power. We can only speculate about the effects of this liberation from his admonition in Chapter 7. Here he speaks to married couples where one spouse is a Christian and the other is not; to single people who want to marry; to gentiles and Jews who had become Christians; and finally to slaves who had become believers. It is clear from Paul's message that some felt Christ had liberated them to leave their unbelieving partner, or to flee their bondage as slaves, or to adopt Jewish customs or gentile ways. It was easy to see how misunderstanding their freedom in Christ could cause a huge disruption in Christian families and in the church, leading to chaos. Paul speaking to each of these life situations gives the same exhortation, summed up in verse 17: "Each person should retain the place in life that the Lord assigned to him and to which God has called him." He then reiterates in verse 20, "Each one should remain in the situation he was in when God called him." Then, finally, one more time in verse 20, just in case the point was still not clear: "Brothers, each man, as responsible to God, should remain in the situation God called him to." Paul uses the language of a military assignment here. God has assigned each of us a place in life, and we are to remain at our post until given orders otherwise.

We can all relate to the confusion that the Apostle was addressing here. No doubt, many of us have felt ambivalence toward the circumstances of our lives at one time or another. We have wondered if this confusion was a sign from God that we should change our circumstances. Fortunately, God's word here is not equivocal: our vacillation is not a sign to leave but on the contrary a sign to remain steadfast at our post. When we are obedient and determined to remain steadfast, we eventually find our situation clarifying. Usually it becomes clear that we are to stay, but sometimes it becomes equally clear that we are to leave. God is not a God of confusion, so if we are confused, it is best to assume God has not yet spoken His final word and to stay put.

I discovered this passage many years ago while preaching through I Corinthians. It was at a time when I was feeling very hesitant about my ministry, wondering if that feeling was the sign from God that it was time to go. I now realize that our church was in a time of transition from a pastoral church to a program church, and I was feeling the intense stress and confusion attendant with that transition. I was in the process of updating my résumé and seriously looking at other ministry opportunities when God spoke to me in a dream one night.

In the dream I was in a house (which, incidentally, I later found out is a dream-language symbol of one's life). There was no door in the house, which disturbed me. I searched and finally found the back door, but it was boarded up. At first, I felt trapped and panicky but then became calm and felt it was ok. Then I woke up. As I reflected on the meaning at the time, it seemed the dream was in response to the restlessness and sense of being trapped that I had been feeling in my ministry. With my résumé updating and job searching, I was looking for a back door out of my ministry. But the eventual calm I experienced seemed like God telling me to stay put, to remain, as Paul had told the Corinthians . . . to trust that He would let me know when it was time to go. Until then, I was to rest in the knowledge that I was in His hands. Thereafter, whenever I felt restless, and I did on many occasions, I accepted that this was not a call from God to leave, but perhaps a sign that there was something else I needed to look at. I determined to stay in my pastorate, erring on the side of remaining not leaving, until God made it clear that my call was concluded. This was not always easy, but the alternative was to be whipsawed with feelings of ambivalence every time things got difficult. I ended up staying for 35 years, and the last 10 years were the happiest and most fruitful of all. During that time the church launched many exciting and effective ministries under many gifted leaders. The church ministered to a wide geographical area and saw many people won to Christ and discipled. We underwent several major building campaigns creating a modern, state-of-the-art campus in a beautiful traditional building. We started a satellite church 5 miles away. We experienced times of awe-inspiring worship week after week.

On a personal note, my wife and I were able to disciple many young couples. She was able to have a productive ministry with young mothers, as well as have a professional career outside the home. Our three daughters were able to graduate from the local (excellent) high school. Later they were each married in that church. I got to walk each of them down the aisle of the church in which they were baptized and confirmed. I shudder to think what would have happened if I had left before it was time to go. I would have missed so much of what God had planned. When it *was* time to go, the congregation celebrated our ministry with the largest gathering ever held at the local country club. Both in a marriage and in a ministry, the words of poet Robert Browning are true: "Grow old along with me, the best is yet to be, the last of life for which the first was made." Now we know that it is not always possible to remain, but if you can, there is much blessing to be gained by staying.

OTHER REASONS FOR STAYING

In addition to Paul's wise and practical counsel to remain, consider the following reasons for staying.

Fruitful ministry. The average pastoral stay is increasing, now approaching 10 years, but that is still short. This is especially so if we consider that a replant takes 7 to 10 years, and often longer. With longevity, you get to see leaders raised up and ministries launched that you could never have dreamed of earlier. And over time, if you are committed to growing yourself, you simply get better at what you do. Your skills and your confidence in leading improve with age.

Family stability. The further along in schooling a child gets, the more disruptive a relocation can be. A spouse's career may also be disrupted by a premature move.

Increased spiritual authority in the church. Over time the spiritual authority of a pastor accrues as you faithfully serve your flock and as more people place themselves under your leadership. Believe it or not, eventually you will have to strive to give authority away so as not to gather too much and possibly abuse it.

Increased influence in the local community. As you live out your witness in the community in words and service, you often become the unofficial town chaplain, ministering to many people who will never enter your church.

A deep bonding with the congregation. You may get to baptize or marry the children of those you baptized or married a generation earlier. It is hard to describe the deep joy and blessing we pastors experience as we walk with our flock over many years, through crises, milestones, rites of passages, and celebrations.

REASONS FOR DEPARTING

In pastoral ministry, unlike in marriage, we pastors are not required to make a lifelong commitment to our congregation. Without such vows, there may be legitimate reasons for parting ways with a church. Here are some that I have seen.

Persistent resistance. It is possible that even after several years the leadership persistently resists your ministry. After you have exhausted all your efforts to lead the church forward, if you are still being stymied by those in authority, it is probably time to leave. Jesus advised his disciples to shake the dust off their feet and move on if they were not welcomed in a town (Luke 10:10-11). We know from Paul's experience in both Corinth (Acts 18:6-7) and Ephesus (Acts 19:8-9) that there comes a time to leave and that to stay longer just subjects the pastor to abuse.

No results. After about 10 years, if you have not seen the revitalization you felt called to lead, it probably is not going to happen. It is Overseed's experience ministering in New England that 10 years is a fair amount of time. The lack of renewal may not be due to the congregation's resistance but simply to the demographics of the church or the community or to the lack of human resources needed to bring the church back. Not every church can be reborn. Sometimes it is easier for a church to die than to live.

Family matters. When you and your family are battle weary, to stay on in the face of resistance or lack of results may cause harm. Your first ministry is always to your family. Similarly, when your extended family is located elsewhere and the desire to be near parents is strong, you may want to choose family over flock. God's call is usually natural and in a context that makes sense.

Test the Spirits

Even in situations like those described above, when the reasons for leaving are compelling, it is important to "test the spirits." ("Dear friends, do not believe every spirit, but test the spirits to see whether they are from God," I John 4:1.) God speaks in many ways, most clearly through the Scriptures, but also through his Holy Spirit directly to our spirits as believers. In my experience a sense of restlessness or general unease or anxiety is often a way that God uses to get my attention. These feelings are like the warning lights on the dashboard of a car. Many times the warning lights are fairly routine and innocuous, like "change oil" or "check engine," but sometimes they are dire warnings of impending disaster, like "low oil pressure." It is important to pay attention to these and to take the proper action.

Sometimes the sense of restlessness or anxiety is like a burglar alarm. We had a lot of experience with these because the parsonage was just a short block from the downtown business district. In the summer with windows open, we would frequently hear alarms go off in the middle of the night. Almost invariably, they were false alarms that went on and on until finally someone shut them off. I would complain as I pulled the pillow over my ears, "Why can't someone fix that darn thing?" It never occurred to me that maybe someone was really breaking into a store and I should call the police. The restlessness, dread, and anxiety we experience are like alarms going off in our spirits. Often, as with burglar alarms, we falsely assume that there's no real problem—the anxiety is just routine, or our worry is mistaken—and the alarm will soon be silent. And most of the time that is the case. However, if the alarm signals do not go away, maybe it really is a warning from God that something is wrong.

So how do we "test the spirits"? Here are some thoughts:

1. Pray on your own and with friends or colleagues who can help you discern God's will.

2. Seek counseling, either career counseling or therapy, if the issue is more emotional in nature.

3. Take a sabbatical. If you have been in your ministry 10 years or more, you have earned a sabbatical. By definition, a sabbatical comes after 6 years, in the 7th year of ministry. Realistically, in a small church a pastor may have to settle for an extra week or two of study or retreat time.

4. Ask yourself if you still have the "fire in the belly." If not, then perhaps you have fulfilled your calling at this church. Some replant pastors may be unintentional interim or transitional pastors, whose calling is to lead a church back to health and then turn it over to someone else to pastor. They then move on to another church in need of replanting. That may be your role. Paul wrote that he planted and Apollos watered, but God gave the increase.

5. Are there some deep-seated, unresolved issues in the church that need to be healed? There may be dark spiritual strongholds. Is the church willing to face them and address them? If not, that may be God's way of leading you on.

6. Revisit your job description. Is it still a good fit with your gifts and strengths? If not, ask your leadership to rewrite

your job description so that your main responsibilities are the things you do best. Then bring in volunteers or paid staff with gifts that complement yours. I speak from experience here. About 25 years into my ministry, I was feeling burned out. For about a year I frequently thought about resigning, but with many good things happening in the church, and kids in college, I knew the time for a drastic move was all wrong. With the help of my leadership (and my wife), I rewrote my job description, and the church hired a part-time administrator from within our congregation. This person eventually came on full-time to manage our staff, oversee our budgeting process, and supervise our programing. As a result, the last 10 years of my ministry were by far the happiest and most fruitful. Acts 6 is a good example of leaders revamping job descriptions and delegating authority to others.

7. Consider the timing. Would a move now disrupt my family? Would a move jeopardize other staff members? Is there a major building project in the works that my leaving would harm? Is there a succession plan in place, or would my departure cause major disruption? Is there conflict or failure on my part that I need to resolve before I go?

If You Are Asked to Leave

Sometimes it is not possible to stay. You may be forced to resign through no fault of your own. Remember that being a replant pastor is like being a missionary, only in this case your church is the mission field. We are not shocked that missionaries are sometimes asked to leave the country they are serving in, and sometimes it happens with replant pastors, too. In such a case, be prepared to safeguard your ministry and above all your family. The following are some ways to do that.

1. Understand the terms of your call as stated in your contract so you can negotiate the best severance package.

Ask for salary commensurate with your time of service. Also, ask for health insurance coverage until you secure a new position. If you are living in church housing, ask to be able to stay for a reasonable amount of time.

2. Ask those who strongly supported your ministry to write any reference or recommendation letters.

3. If you belong to a denomination, ask them to help in the negotiation. However, be aware that denominations may side with the church and not the pastor since the cost of losing a church is far greater to the denomination than losing a pastor.

4. It is better to resign than to be fired.

5. If possible, have a vocation that you can fall back on to provide for your family. Remember Paul was a tent maker. Historically in Judaism, rabbis were always bi-vocational, first so they could minister free of charge if needed, but second so they could provide for their families in times of persecution. The late professor Henry Brooks of Andover-Newton Theological School was always both a professor and a pastor, coming from a long line of African American pastors who were also always bi-vocational. He articulated the tradition in the black church of the necessity of providing in times of economic difficulty or racial discrimination. Before I entered the ministry, I earned a degree in counseling and was prepared to earn my living that way if necessary. I recall a rather tense budget meeting early in my ministry when one difficult church member threatened, "Remember, pastor, we can cut your salary." I replied calmly, "If you do that, I'll start a counseling practice." Counseling was the last thing I wanted to do, but just saying it was enough to end that bullying tactic.

6. In the 20th century, pastors with parsonages often owned a vacation cottage so they would have a place to retire to or, between churches, a place to house their family. In the

many small towns or rural areas where parsonages are still provided, home ownership of some sort may still be a desirable goal, if possible.

7. Have a financial plan. The words of John Wesley apply: "Earn all you can; save all you can; give away all you can." Saving for the future gives you freedom to step away from your ministry if you have to and to retire when you want to. If you are forced to continue working out of financial necessity after you no longer have the stamina or passion, your ministry is no longer a labor of love but servitude.

8. Swallow your pride. Sometimes the reason for overstaying is not financial but an inflated ego. If a pastor feels the church "just can't do without me," it is probably time to leave. When this is the attitude, it only hurts the church.

The Apostle Paul writes in II Corinthians 2:14 that "God always leads us in triumphal procession in Christ." The image is of a Roman triumph in which a conquering hero leads his captives in a victory parade. Paul means that we are Christ's captives and he is always leading us forward in His victory. I do not believe Christ will lead us backward in failure. Of course, we may fail, and often do, but Christ will not cause us to fail. If we are walking in obedience to him, we will not have to leave in failure.

I have two final words of advice for pastors contemplating resigning: First, *"All's well that ends well."* In other words, finish strong, while the congregation still wants you. Do not undo years of effective ministry by staying too long. And second, *"When you get to the end of your journey, stop."* Know when you have accomplished your mission. There will always be more goals, but if you can honestly leave your ministry in a healthy state and it is time to go, then depart and allow the Lord to open a new chapter in your life and in the life of your church.

18

Reinvention for the Long Haul

As a church is revitalized, it changes, and so does the pastor's role in that church. This is especially true as the size culture of the church changes. When a church grows from family size to pastoral size, it relies more and more on pastoral leadership because it becomes too big to lead itself. Authority is more centralized in the pastor, and only he or she knows everyone. A frequent complaint from members nostalgic for the family size is, "I don't know everyone any more," or "Who are all these new people?" These folks will resist the transition and possibly even try to sabotage renewal because they feel left behind or left out. Others will see their authority and control diminishing as the church grows larger.

Pastors sometimes become victims of their own success as a church becomes healthy and spiritually mature. They inadvertently become bottlenecks as members look to them for leadership and permission to proceed on all matters. If the pastor of a pastoral size church continues to function as before, the revitalization will stall and he or she will probably burn out. As the church grows and is transformed, the pastor must continually reinvent his or her role and functioning to avoid being overwhelmed with the demands of burgeoning ministry.

Reinvention may be a deliberate, thought-out process as a pastor reads books about church dynamics and attends seminars on leadership. It may come about as a pastor studies relevant biblical texts on leading and serving, like Exodus 18 (Jethro's counsel to Moses) and Acts 6 (the choosing of deacons). These passages record crisis moments when leaders are besieged by the burdens of ministry and realize that they must change the way they lead. Reinvention often happens that way, as pastors experience and respond to crisis moments in pastoral ministry.

I recall one evening in my ministry years ago. Our church had grown from family to pastoral size, but I had not reinvented my role. I was still trying to shepherd everyone as I had when I first arrived. It was my practice to visit every newcomer to the church. That meant I was out routinely three evenings a week meeting visitors, attending committee meetings, and leading Bible studies. On this particular night I was frantically driving around a neighborhood in the dark trying to find the home of a new young family. These were the days before GPS and cell phones. I prayed that I'd find their street sign or mailbox, or at least a pay phone. I finally arrived almost an hour late, extremely frustrated and apologetic. On my way home, I had a "Jethro moment," only it wasn't my father-in-law but the Holy Spirit who spoke to me. I had to change my ways. The clear message was that I would no longer be able to provide that previous level of direct, one-on-one pastoral care and that I was robbing my young children of precious time with their dad. The result was the beginning of our small group ministry. The ministry developed slowly, with fits and starts, but over the years small groups grew into one of our most important ministries. Hundreds of people were evangelized and discipled in various types of small groups.

At first I recruited, trained, and supervised all the group leaders. Eventually, I developed a lay volunteer to do this, and later we hired a part-time, then a full-time staff person to oversee all small group ministries. It was under his skilled and prayerful leadership that we were able to have more than 95 small groups meeting regularly and caring for about 1,000 members.

Because of the demographics of our church setting, many of the newcomers over the years were couples. Some moved to the area for jobs in the nearby high-tech, bio-med, and financial headquarters. Others with young children came because of the excellent public and private schools. Throughout my 35-year pastorate, my wife and I were continuously leading couples small groups. She and I work well as a team and felt we could have the greatest impact ministering together with other couples. Having both spouses present and growing in a group each week made the discipleship process holistic and efficient.

As a church moves beyond the family size, the pastor functions as the "gate keeper," with newcomers initially connecting to the church through him or her. But unless there is a vehicle or system for helping new people form relationships with others in the church, they will typically drift away after a few months. Because newcomers are first bonded to the pastor, it makes sense for the pastor to gather them into a small group that he or she leads. When our church was pastoral size, this is what my wife and I did with couples being drawn in. We usually met together for a year before either branching or turning over leadership to an apprentice leader. By that time, the group members were bonded to one another, not just to me, and would likely stay in the church family. It was so encouraging to see groups sitting together on Sunday mornings and exhibiting evidence of true Christian community.

When functioning well, small groups will provide a span of care that far exceeds what a pastor can provide. One example stands out in my mind. A young couple had experienced a miscarriage, but it was several days before I was able to schedule a pastoral visit. When I called, the husband told me that their couples small group had surrounded them with visits, prayers, and meals, and that with this support they were grieving their loss well. It wasn't necessary for me to visit. Every pastor dreams of hearing this.

Granted, the process didn't always work smoothly or predictably. As Dr. Roberta Hestenes (the "Mother of Small Groups") says, "Small groups are messy!" But when I retired, I estimated that about one-third of our thousand-member church had been in a small group with either me or my wife or both of us.

Not only does a pastor's reinvention involve a process for assimilating new believers. The pastor must also revisit and reinvent his or her work priorities. This is certainly the lesson of Acts 6, when the Apostles realized they could no longer do all the work they did at first. They wisely prioritized their ministry, spending most of their time "in prayer and the ministry of the word." I came to believe that the ministry of preaching was my most important activity. I typically spent about 20 hours a week in sermon preparation, including praying about the text and for my congregation. After preaching, my priority was developing leaders. It took discipline and intentionality to carve out the time for fellowshipping with, discipling, and training leaders. The clamor of all the other demands of pastoral ministry meant that I had to make this a real priority. But this was part of the necessary reinvention I had to undergo to keep pace with God's movement in our church. Vital, responsive ministry in a church over the long haul requires that we pastors continue growing, and reinventing our roles, as our ministry grows.

HEALTHY BOUNDARIES

It was said of Moses at the end of his life that "his eyes were not weak, nor his strength gone" (Deuteronomy 34:7). May that be said of all replant pastors at the close of their ministries. Establishing healthy habits in life and ministry is essential, and good boundaries are the key. By boundaries, we mean those

215

usually unwritten guidelines that help us know how to proceed in our personal and professional lives. These are the common sense practices that we learned in Bible school or seminary, but learning and doing are often two different things. (Some of the following is adapted from *Healthy Boundaries for Clergy and Spiritual Teachers*, published by the FaithTrust Institute.)

Relationship Boundaries

All pastors, not just replant pastors, need to scrupulously avoid any inappropriate interactions with his or her parishioners or people outside the church. These can destroy a ministry, a personal life or family, and even a church. It is imperative that pastors understand, establish, and maintain relationship boundaries. Such boundaries protect congregants from the abuse of the power that pastors have due to their leadership positions. Boundaries also protect pastors from false accusations. Boundaries are not meant to block authenticity and warmth in personal relationships, and properly applied, they won't. Rather than shackling us, they free us in our work as spiritual leaders.

Boundaries help us as pastors or ministry leaders maintain clear professional relationships. They help us discern when and when not to participate in a given activity. They give us some distance and perspective when people's problems seem overwhelming. And they signal to others that it is safe to trust us.

Here are some guardrails to put in place so you do not cross boundaries inappropriately and end up in danger.

- Be aware of your own needs and find godly, and appropriate, ways of meeting them.
- Ask yourself if your actions are in the best interests of the other person, or do they only satisfy your needs?
- Establish a system of accountability with a mentor, spiritual director, or colleague.

- Understand that boundaries are not always easy to discern, and that often there are no clear guidelines for the best action to take.
- Be careful when accepting gifts from church members. Be certain you are not expected to reciprocate. Find a way to decline gifts that are inappropriate.
- Never discuss your own marriage or personal problems with those who come to you for help. Find someone who is both competent and trustworthy outside your congregation with whom to discuss your problems.

Counseling members of your congregation.
Counseling was traditionally a major part of a pastor's job description. The typical pastor, with little or no training in counseling, was expected to listen to parishioners' personal relational or emotional problems and then offer advice, exhort from the Scriptures, and pray for the counselees. As valid as that may have been in a bygone era, that is not counseling. And in today's anxious climate, such practices expose a pastor to real danger. Even though I have an advanced degree and was trained in pastoral counseling, I do not counsel nor do I recommend that pastors counsel, especially not members of the opposite sex. In my observation, many if not most pastoral moral failures occur as a result of a counseling experience. Counseling is the most emotionally intimate contact a pastor engages in with his or her congregation. The fact that far more women than men seek out counseling from their pastor, and the help they seek often involves their marriages, makes the practice highly problematic for male pastors.

Do not offer a counseling ministry at all unless you are properly trained and licensed as a counselor. Don't deceive yourself: One or two pastoral counseling courses in Bible school or seminary does not qualify you to counsel. A better approach is to meet once or twice with individuals who come to you so you can hear their story, truly empathize with them, offer scriptural guidance, pray with them, and then refer them to a professional counselor. You can continue to check in with them to see the progress they are making. This form of "support" counseling is most appropriate.

Of course, it is important that a pastor be accessible to the congregation to listen intently and to support them in their struggles, but do not undertake therapeutic counseling unless you are trained. Locate two or three trained and licensed counselors in your area and get to know them. Talk to other pastors who have used them. At least one should be a Christian for your parishioners who insist on going to a Christian counselor. However, in my opinion, whether or not they are a Christian is secondary to whether they are competent and can help your people find emotional or relational healing.

Meeting with members of the opposite sex. With regard to meetings, be strongly advised with what I believe are common-sense, clear guidelines for meeting with members of the opposite sex to whom we are not related:

- Do not meet members of the opposite sex, except during office hours. When meeting during office hours, always meet with them on church property, not in your home or their home. Make sure others are present in the building when you are meeting. Meet in a room that has a door with glass panels or leave the door ajar.
- Do not meet members of the opposite sex in public settings such as restaurants, even if it is for church business. Others observing you may assume the worst.
- Do not travel alone with members of the opposite sex, even if it is on church business.
- Be aware of any sexual feelings toward congregants or staff members. Because ministry can be relationally intimate, it is not uncommon to have feelings of attraction toward others

218

you are serving or working with. Be very scrupulous in acknowledging these feelings to yourself, to your mentor, even to your spouse, but never to the person who is the object of these feelings and never to a congregant or staff member.

- If a congregant or staff member engages in sexualized behavior toward you, never respond in kind. Maintain your role as spiritual leader and consult with your mentor. Be careful to document any such activity.
- Be alert to your potential for co-dependency in relationships with your congregants. The following checklist can alert you to the potential for danger:
  - ✓ Do you experience inappropriate excitement in one-on-one meetings with a congregant?
  - ✓ Have you ever confided in a congregant about aspects of your marriage?
  - ✓ Have you ever called or emailed a congregant because of an emotional need to be in contact with them?
  - ✓ Do you ever create situations in which congregants take care of you?
  - ✓ Do you ever use the pulpit to share too much about your own problems?

  If you answer yes to any of these, you probably need to change how you exercise your leadership in the church.

Transference. *Transference* is defined as "confusing the feelings you have for one person with feelings you have for another." In other words, does that young woman in your congregation remind you of an old girlfriend? Has that older gentleman become a father figure reminding you of the father you longed for but never had? Parishioners often experience transference in relationship with a pastor, confusing their feelings for their spouse with their feelings for their pastor. Again, be alert and honest with yourself, with God and with your mentor.

Pastors today are very aware of the issue of hugging and touching others. Touch is an important part of pastoral ministry, but it can also be an inappropriate boundary crossing. As pastors, we need to ask the following: Is this a transference instance, where my feelings or the other person's feelings have sexual undertones? Is this touch in their best interests, or is it about my needs? Is there a better way to convey caring and warmth?

Friendship boundaries. Maintaining healthy friendships in a church is part of having relationship boundaries. If you stay for a long time in a church, you will inevitably face the challenge of having close friends in your congregation. There is a long-standing debate between those who insist that it is not possible to have close friends among your congregants and those who say it is. I think both are right. But because it is hard to be someone's pastor and friend, it is important to build such friendships slowly over time. Mutual trust and testing of the relationship is important. Even Jesus was careful in trusting himself to people, as John 2:24 reminds us, "because He knew what was in men's hearts." Many pastors and their families have been deeply hurt by betrayal because they moved too quickly to trust themselves to people they did not adequately know.

That said, the small group setting is an excellent and safe environment for a pastor to form friendships with members of the congregation. A weekly small group meeting provides adequate time for a pastor to know and be known by parishioners, a few at a time. Part of every small group experience ought to be personal sharing of ideas, beliefs, feelings, and concerns, all at an appropriate level; boundaries are in place. Over the course of my long-time pastorate, my wife and I were in small group community with hundreds of members of our church. Many lifelong friendships were forged around small group circles, in fellowship, prayer, shared tasks, study of the Word, caring in crisis, and, yes, lots of fun. Although my closest friendships have always been with those outside my church, my small group experience has yielded a

220

warmth and deep affection for so many with whom I have shared group life.

Pornography. So much has been said and written about the destructive effects of pornography, but it continues to ruin marriages, ministries, and souls. No man or woman is immune to the sexual temptation of pornographic images or words. The most straightforward way to deal with it is to block it on your computer, TV, and phone. If it is readily available, anyone can be tempted; will power will not work. Be accountable to your spouse and to others whom you trust.

It cannot be stated too strongly that maintaining appropriate relationship boundaries in the ministry is essential if we are to honor God and our families and fulfill our pastoral responsibilities for the long haul. "Flee from sexual immorality" (I Corinthians 6:18) is the strong boundary language of the word of God. While we believe undeniably in a gospel of grace and redemption, failure in this regard can and has destroyed innumerable ministries, churches, marriages, families, and lives forever.

WORK BOUNDARIES

Pastors have more discretion over their work schedules than just about any other profession, so we have nobody to blame but ourselves if we cannot manage our time. The ability to set good work boundaries is essential to being able to stay vital in your ministry for the long run.

Work boundaries start with a comprehensive job description and clear expectations of what is required of you. If you are just starting in ministry, negotiate this at the beginning. If you are already in ministry without a written job description, take this up with your leadership.

If you are in full-time ministry you should expect to work roughly the same number of hours that the average person in your congregation works, plus the time for the average commute. I

consistently worked a 50-55 hour week, as most of my
congregation had 40-hour work weeks and commuted an hour
each way to work.

Delegating Ministry

Delegating is not only biblical (Ephesians 4:11-13), it is also
essential if a pastor is to avoid burnout in the ministry. Delegating
is part of the reinvention process that pastors must embrace if they
are to keep from becoming an obstacle to the transforming work of
the Holy Spirit in his church. A pastor in either a family size or a
pastoral size church must continually be raising up ministry leaders
and turning ministries over to them. Otherwise, he or she will
become a bottleneck for ministries and deny the laity opportunities
to discover and exercise their gifts. Both family and pastoral size
churches can easily become too dependent on the pastor, and the
pastor can become codependent in this relationship. When a
church and pastor stay stuck in this unhealthy codependency, it
limits the development of a healthy "body life" through the gifting
of the Holy Spirit. Be intentional about reinventing your role as
pastor and delegating ministry to those in your church who are
gifted and called. Preaching and teaching on spiritual gifts and on
the Ephesians 4 pattern of church life are so important, especially
given how much space is devoted to these matters in the New
Testament.

Find ways to save time in your ministry because you cannot
do everything you are asked to do. In Acts 6, we see that the
Apostles realized they could not do all that was expected. They
had to decide what was essential in their calling and delegate to
others what was not. Here are some areas in which you may need
to decide what is essential in your ministry and what is not.

Visitation. Early in a pastoral tenure, visits from the pastor
are essential. In the honeymoon phase, you are getting to know
your flock and building trust. As time goes on, however, this is a
ministry that others can help with. Decide to delegate some of the

visitation to those parishioners who have gifts of mercy, helps, service, and hospitality. I believe that, over time, much (but not all) of the pastoral care ministry can be turned over to trained, gifted lay people. (The Stephen Ministry is a great tool for training and equipping people for this caregiving.)

Weddings. Weddings are among the most joyful events in the lives of our congregations. It is a great honor to share in these rites of passage with our people. They are also wonderful occasions for proclaiming the gospel to those outside your church. The longer you serve a congregation, the more opportunities you have to act as the unofficial chaplain of your community and to perform weddings among those outside your membership. I sometimes did up to 15 weddings a year, including those of townspeople who did not attend our church. For Protestants, we realize from the Scriptures that marriage is a common grace, not limited to Christians but a blessing from God for all men and women since the Creation. I was comfortable conducting the weddings of friends who were not part of the church, as long as I was marrying two Christians or two non-Christians. Preparing a couple for a wedding can take a lot of time. I found it made sense to ask the couples to do their premarital counseling through a "Prepare and Enrich" program, or something similar. We trained several lay people in our church to teach it, and we then required all couples to take it. I was then free to meet with the couple to get to know them, to share scriptural principles of marriage with them, and to plan the wedding.

I also learned to schedule wedding rehearsals for late on the afternoon of the day before the wedding. If there was any reluctance about that timing, I would gently remind the couple that the rehearsal was for their benefit not mine and that late afternoon was the time that I was available. This saved another evening out for me. I never had pushback on this. The reception following a wedding is the longest part of this milestone event. Pastors must decide if they should spend an additional four hours at a wedding reception on a Saturday given all the preparation needed to be ready for worship and preaching on Sunday. I often suggested to a couple that my wife and I would prefer to attend the rehearsal dinner, typically a smaller gathering in a more intimate setting the evening before the ceremony. The rehearsal dinner allowed us to get better acquainted with the family and friends of the couple (and it was a nice evening out with my wife). It was usually an acceptable alternative for the couple to have us attend that event rather than the wedding reception.

Feeding the sheep. The pastor as shepherd is one of the richest image in the Scriptures. Our Lord tells the Apostle Peter three times to "feed my sheep" (John 21). But what exactly does it mean to feed the sheep? In family and pastoral size churches, you are not only the feeder but can also find yourself becoming the food. I confess that in the early days of my ministry, I thought that offering myself, my time, my love, my efforts to meet my congregation's every need were the food I was to give. As a result, I devoted an inordinate amount of time responding to the needs and demands of my flock. I was spending more time than I could afford with the neediest people in the church, with little to show for it except my exhaustion. When I shared my struggle with my mentor, he pointed out that we are not the food; the Word of God is the food that we are to give our flocks. He challenged me to spend more time on my sermons and on the Bible study I was leading and less time running around the parish trying to meet everyone's needs and demands. That lesson alone probably did more to help revitalize my church than anything else. It is the Word of God "living and active" (Hebrews 4:12) that nourishes and transforms lives, not the pastor.

RHYTHM NOT BALANCE

I am indebted to author Mark Buchanan for the distinction between rhythm and balance, and I believe it is more than semantics. To me, rhythm is a more helpful concept than the popular notion of trying to find balance in our lives. Rhythm is a more natural phenomenon. We naturally have a rhythm to our days, weeks, months, and seasons. It is important to discover your rhythm in each of these time units if you are to minister for the long haul.

Daily Rhythm

Poet William Blake (1757–1827) said, "Think in the morning. Act in the noon. Eat in the evening. Sleep in the night." This is still a good rhythm to follow. Each of us must find and follow our own rhythms. As an example, let me share mine.

Early morning is the time I always spent reading the Bible, praying, and journaling—and still do. I am an early riser, and I found that the quiet in the house before others were awake was a very fruitful time for my own personal growth. For years after our children were up and dressed but before they caught the school bus, we would read Scripture and pray with them, even if it was only for a few moments. This meant that I was not available for early morning meetings, although I did occasionally make exceptions when early morning was the only time available. Likewise, morning office hours were the most productive time for me to meet with staff, to make contact with many people by phone or email, and to organize the work for that day. I found noontime ideal for meeting men in my church for lunch, often at their workplaces. Mid- to late afternoon was, for me, the best time to visit at the hospital or meet people in my office. By then, as my energy was ebbing, I found being with people was energizing. Visiting at the hospital or a nursing home often blessed me more than those I was seeing. Dinners were almost always at home around the family dinner table. (I am thankful to my wife for imposing this discipline on our family's daily rhythm.) Two to three evenings a week were spent at meetings, leading Bible studies or small groups, or visiting new families in the church. In hindsight, I recommend that a pastor not be out more than two evenings a week, especially if he or she has young children. Some churches stack their meetings on the same evening to allow the pastor to touch base with all the committees. Or the pastor can host a meeting at home so he or she can attend but not have to go out.

Weekly Rhythm

The Sabbath. The Fourth Commandment is the one commandment that is in our favor, and pastors are wise to observe it. The problem for pastors is that our busiest day is the Sabbath, so we need to find another day to observe as our Sabbath. Find the day that works for you and your family, as well as for your personal work-rest rhythm. For me, observing the Sabbath was (and still remains) wrapped up in two great truths: doing everything in six days, and looking forward to something special every week.

One day off per week is realistic. But take that one day off! Be ruthless in observing a Sabbath. If possible, screen your calls or get out of town on that day. Be truthful about how essential you are: you really are not on call 24/7. In an emergency most people will call 911, not you. When all is said and done and your life is over, your children will be blessed that you put them before your ministry.

Getting everything done in six days. My practical understanding of the Sabbath was shaped first by my childhood family Sabbath practice and later by my early years in full-time ministry. Then, for the first time in my life, I sensed the need for a Sabbath myself. I realized the importance of distinguishing between the end of one week and the beginning of the next. Whenever my weeks began running into each other, I would begin to experience a low-grade depression and fatigue. My life and work became joyless. The emotional output of pastoral ministry was such that I needed to make a clean break between weeks. By observing the Sabbath, we get that break that we desperately need.

226

The Hebrew word for Sabbath means, among other things, "to stop"—stop the work you have been doing for six days and do something else. So I had to get my work done each week and not let it carry over into the next. It was very important to return my phone calls and clear my desk each Friday afternoon. This way I could enjoy a Friday evening with my family and spend Saturday making final preparations for Sunday. I had to get everything done in six days. Having the weekly deadline of a sermon to prepare certainly helped. In many occupations, work can spill over into the next week, but a pastor cannot postpone the sermon for another day.

Doing everything we need to do in six days means the Sabbath is truly free. This is exactly what God commanded the Israelites to do in Exodus 20:9-10. "Six days you shall labor and do ALL your work, but the seventh is a Sabbath to the Lord your God." This notion of finishing each week's work in the allotted time was liberating for me. Of course, there were many occasions when it did not happen. Except for the weekly preaching deadline, much of church ministry is imprecise and fluid. Overall, though, having as my goal the completion of each week was healthy for my family and me. I was living in gratitude to the Lord of the Sabbath for this great gift to all humanity, the Fourth Commandment. It is a gift we *need*, and we ignore it at our peril.

Here's what my weekly rhythm looked like on my six days of work. Tuesday to Thursday mornings were for me best spent in the office leading the work of the parish. Afternoons were spent visiting or meeting people in my office. Friday mornings were sermon study time, which I did at the small office I had set up in the parsonage because there were too many distractions at the church office. Friday afternoons I spent at the church returning phone calls and replying to correspondence. I tried to conclude my office workweek by 5:00 on Friday afternoon knowing that Saturday and Sunday would be totally focused on being ready to preach and lead worship. Most Saturdays were given over to my final sermon preparation. Saturday night I tried to be home in order to spend time in prayer after my kids were in bed. We rarely attended social events on Saturday evenings; it was home time. And then, there's Sunday. Enough said.

I always maintained my own schedule rather than have my secretary keep my calendar. Knowing my daily and weekly rhythms allowed me to do each part of my work at my most advantageous time. Of course, as we know, any given day or week in ministry can be interrupted and dominated by tragedies or crises. Then, the routine schedule goes out the window.

Looking forward to something special each week. When my children were small, my Sabbath was from Sunday afternoon to Monday night when we tucked them into bed. Fortunately, our church never had a tradition of a Sunday night service, and I was not about to start one. I believe it is important for church families to be at home together at the start of their school and work weeks. Our Sunday afternoon ritual was to take family rides. It did not matter where as long as it was inexpensive. We spent a lot of time in museums with free passes from our library, wandering malls, or walking on the beach, especially in the winter when they are deserted. We had three children close in age, and so it was hard for them all to agree on what our Sunday ride would be, so I took a page out of my youth ministry playbook. We would tell the kids that the destination was a secret; they would not know where we were going until we got there. We called them Mystery Rides. Everyone loves a mystery, and the mystery prevented the arguments. Once the kids were back in school on Monday, my wife and I were able to spend the rest of the Sabbath together. Her job as a part-time freelance book editor enabled us to do this.

I grew up in a fairly traditional Christian home where the Sabbath was spent attending church and Sunday school, having a big Sunday dinner at home, and then taking a Sunday afternoon drive, often to visit cousins and my grandmother. Frequently, the outing included a stop on the way home for ice cream. The only prohibited behavior ever imposed was going to the movie theater on Sunday, and that was only for a brief period when I was in middle school. Sundays were a happy time, and I cherish the fond memories of the family being together and enjoying small adventures.

For the ancient Israelites, the Sabbath must have been such an incredible blessing. Ancient peoples were typically agrarian, engaged in unending toil. The Jews must have eagerly looked forward to the Sabbath as a day to rest, to be with family, to eat and drink, and to worship God. I believe every person needs something to look forward to each week. The Sabbath commands us to live our lives in weeklong segments, anticipating times of physical and spiritual renewal. Having our weekly Mystery Rides meant our children had something to look forward to each week as well. When they were in the middle of a long school week, we could encourage them by saying, "Hang in there—we're going on a Mystery Ride in a few days!"

Seasonal Rhythm

While the calendar year begins in January, the unofficial church year begins for many churches in September. In our church, there were three seasons: fall, winter, and spring. Summer in New England is short and glorious, so our attendance in summer often dropped by half as people vacationed. Committees stopped meeting, Sunday school classes combined, and substitute teachers filled in. Small groups were encouraged to take a hiatus or meet only for occasional fellowship events. My summer schedule was light enough that I was able to spend more time studying, reflecting, and planning. It was also a time for me to read, both defensively for ministry and offensively for personal growth. Summer was also time for family vacations. I had four weeks of vacation, usually taking two in the summer and two other times when my children were on school vacation. Eventually I was given an additional week for study.

I also came to appreciate the rhythm that the traditional church year gives to the work of ministry. The church year begins with Advent, the four Sundays before Christmas. Although it was not a strong tradition in our church, we observed it because it was an antidote to the stress of the Christmas season. Observing Advent meant it was easier for our staff and leaders to plan services in advance. It made it easier for me to plan sermons. We developed fun family devotionals for our people to use in their homes. We found that Advent and Christmas were a time when unchurched people attended in greater numbers, and offering family-friendly Christmas traditions was a helpful way to connect with them. Observing Advent also helped us return the focus of Christmas to Christ and to centering our lives in Him.

We then began making more of the season of Lent. Lent derives from the word *lengthen*, referring to the longer hours of daylight in the late winter and spring. In northern latitudes it was the perfect time for an increased discipleship focus, which was the original purpose for Lent. Again, the tradition of the church year provided a pattern and structure for worship and preaching. It also allowed us an opportunity to introduce "new" worship traditions, such as Ash Wednesday and Maundy Thursday. Both of these services have ancient roots in Christian history but have often been jettisoned by evangelicals who don't recognize their discipleship value.

In addition to the church year, I also needed to pay attention to my own natural seasonal rhythm, especially in late winter. Perhaps I am slightly affected by SAD (seasonal affect disorder), but I found it was important for me and for my family to save some vacation time for winter. I once heard Dr. Harold Ockenga, the founder and president of Gordon-Conwell Theological Seminary, tell a group of students that he tried to find a church conference every winter held in a warm sunny place. He was able to combine both work and pleasure in that way. After I had been in my church for 10 years, I persuaded the elders to put a small line item in the budget for winter travel and study. Our first trip was to the Holy Land in February, when the desert is blooming. We also attended several conferences in Southern California. Getaways like these helped this New England pastor stay at my post for the long haul.

I remember the occasion when I convinced my board to grant me one more week of vacation for study. One of the elders objected, "None of us gets 5 weeks off a year; why should you?" I believe the Holy Spirit gave me the answer: "Everyone here works 5 days a week. I work 6 days a week. That means I work 52 more days than you, so you actually get 7 more weeks off than I do." They voted unanimously to give me the extra week study leave. I always tried to use it to keep my mind and spirit fresh. Understanding your rhythms and the rhythms of the seasons is vital to staying healthy emotionally and spiritually for the long journey of replant ministry.

A SPIRITUALLY HEALTHY LIFESTYLE

So much has been written about spiritual health over the last several decades—and over the centuries—that I do not need to repeat it. Nor can I really add anything to this body of devotional literature. To my mind, one of the best books on the subject is Richard Foster's *Celebration of Discipline*. It is one of the clearest and most practical volumes ever written about the Christian spiritual life, and it belongs in the body of classic devotional literature. Simply reproducing the table of contents is helpful:

- *The Inward Disciplines*
    Meditation
    Prayer
    Fasting
    Study

- *The Outward Disciplines*
    - *Simplicity*
    - *Solitude*
    - *Submission*
    - *Service*

- *The Corporate Disciplines*
    - *Confession*
    - *Worship*
    - *Guidance*
    - *Celebration*

The Inward Disciplines are the easiest for pastors to follow; the Outward and Corporate Disciplines are more difficult. Among the Outward Disciplines described by Foster, Solitude and Submission strike me as vital for a pastor in a replant situation. And among the Corporate Disciplines, Confession and Worship are likewise essential. Solitude, submission, confession, and worship are spiritual disciplines that are easy for replants pastors to neglect.

Solitude

Solitude is hard to imagine for a busy pastor with a family, but unless we get alone and listen to God, we will tend to follow our own devices and desires in our ministries. God spoke most clearly to me when I found time and space to get alone with my Bible, my journal, and an open heart. I was able to find several suitable retreat centers within a 25-mile radius of my church. Many of them were Roman Catholic monasteries or convents that opened their doors for private retreats. Many of these places also offered meals and overnight lodging for any donation I was able to make. It was on one such retreat, early in my ministry, that I sensed God spoke to me a word of assurance that sustained me in the long difficult years of the revitalization ministry he called me to. The words were so clear that I wrote them down verbatim and recall them to this day decades later. The Holy Spirit of Jesus said, "If you will honor my name in this church, I will pour out such blessing on your ministry that you won't be able to contain it." At the time, it seemed a far-fetched prophesy for a church that had considered closing its doors or merging with one of the three other Congregational churches in town. Yet nevertheless that is what I heard, and it is what gave me hope that my work was not futile. It was a word I needed to recall when the work was difficult and the opposition was fierce. I needed to remember it when the temptation to soft-peddle the message of Christ in a liberal setting was strong. Though I failed many times to fully honor Christ, God was faithful to honor His part, and we did indeed eventually see such blessing that, in many ways, we were unable to contain it.

Submission

Submission is the other outward spiritual discipline that I would single out from Richard Foster's list. Submission seems to us an unnatural attitude, especially in the early years of ministry when we have limited authority as pastors. It seems we should be trying to gain the power and control needed to lead change. Instead, Foster challenges us to yield up what little power we have. I am not sure that submission is in the vocabulary of most of us as young and inexperienced pastors. It certainly was not in mine.

The early years of a revitalization ministry are all about striving to gain a small measure of authority. As we have noted, small declining churches are fully capable of functioning on their own with minimal leadership from a pastor. A pastor in the first phases of ministry has little authority. Indeed, some of the anxiety a pastor experiences in the early years centers around a sense of powerlessness. I had a recurring dream in my early years in which I would discover that the church leaders were conducting an important meeting and had not told me or invited me. Often it was not a dream but a reality. Another source of anxiety for a new pastor is the fierce opposition and stubborn resistance mustered by

233

the flock. Typically, a pastor has never experienced anything like it, and no class in seminary or Bible school prepared him or her for it. So the notion of submission to the duly appointed authority of the church is foreign to a new pastor, especially if that appointed authority is spiritually weak, or not even Christian. On the contrary, we newly minted pastors expect the leadership to submit to us. However, to be obedient to Christ is to submit to the existing authority, no matter how flawed they are.

Confession

Our Protestant impulses tell us that confession to God is enough, but our experience teaches us that sometimes confession to another person is needed to gain assurance of our forgiveness and break the power of our sin. I encourage the replant pastors that I coach to have someone to whom they can go to unburden their conscience. I usually do not recommend that it be their spouse, as this can be extremely burdensome for a marriage. Instead, I suggest they find someone who is both trustworthy and wise. Trustworthy means someone who is saturated with the grace of God and can with spiritual authority assure them of God's mercy and forgiveness. The measure of a trustworthy person is the feeling that we could tell them anything and they would not judge us. The person must also be competent. In other words, they need to have the wisdom and skill to actually help us and not only listen to us. Some of our acquaintances may be competent, but we do not fully trust them; others may be trustworthy, but we do not feel they could help us. Seek out that competent and trustworthy person to be your confessor.

Worship

When does a pastor worship? I can honestly say that for many years it was not possible for me to worship in my own church on a Sunday morning. Early on in my tenure, our service was very traditional with many components, and I had to lead all of it. I was so focused on getting all the parts right and in order, and then preaching my sermon, that I had little opportunity to focus my heart and mind on God. It was not until later, when we had a skilled and godly worship team and lay elders to assist in leading the service that I was able to relax and enter into full-hearted worship. To compensate for this, my wife and I would periodically spend a day at an Episcopal monastery (yes, they do have monks), where the high liturgy and simple homily from the Scriptures was a beautiful worship experience for us. The setting was an English Gothic chapel with stained glass windows and vaulted ceilings, all of which added a richness and a sense of the timelessness to the experience. We treasured those times of worship and only regret that we now live three hours away from that monastery.

When your pastoral heart is hungry for the Lord, you will find Christ-centered worship in many different settings. Sometimes when I felt spiritually dry, I would worship at a nearby charismatic, Christ-centered Roman Catholic church. This particular service was on Friday nights, so after my small children were tucked in bed and my wife was unwinding from a long week, I would steal away for this prayer service. On more than one occasion, the faithful parishioners and priest would lay hands on me and pray for me. If you, like me, struggle to worship in your own Sunday services, find other opportunities to worship in the midst of your ministry. Do not be the only one in your congregation who does not worship.

A Word About Family Devotions

Family devotions . . . it's a topic that many of us as pastors avoid addressing in sermons because our own record is not so great. Early in my marriage, before we had children, it bothered me that unless I suggested to my wife that we pray together, it never happened. This is not to suggest that my wife was not spiritual, she is, and in fact, her faith and godliness have often been used by the Lord to call me to greater devotion. It was just that I was always the one to initiate any prayer effort. Then it dawned on me that it was actually the biblical expectation that the husband would take the lead. I decided simply to accept this assignment as falling in my job description. From then on, we had a regular practice of praying very briefly before we each went out the door to our respective jobs. We still have this as our practice. Many mornings it is little more than a sentence-long prayer focusing on whatever is uppermost in our minds. I would feel ill prepared for my day if we were to neglect it. I used to envy those pastors who would read the Bible or some devotional literature together with their spouse, but then I realized that was not how it was going work for us.

When my children were little, we would read their children's Bible to them as we put them to bed. Then when they began elementary school, we would read a few verses each morning as they waited for the school bus outside the parsonage. My family devotional plan with my children was very simple: we would start in Genesis and read through the historical literature, then Psalms, and Proverbs. Then we would read selectively from the Prophets and on into the New Testament Gospels, Acts, and Epistles. I was selective depending on their age. It was easier to do a quick edit as I read rather than to explain what a harlot or a eunuch was. The amount we read was determined by how much time we had after getting ready and before the school bus arrived. Sometimes it was 10 minutes and sometimes it was 1 minute. Then we would send them out the door, placing our hands on their heads and giving them a quick Trinitarian blessing. We read the Bible that way for years until they were in middle school and asked if they could just read on their own. The Trinitarian blessings still go on, though. Every time we see them and take our leave, we place our hands on them, bless them, their spouses, and our grandchildren. By God's mercy, all three of our children are well married, blessing their own children, active in their churches, and walking with Christ. My cup is full.

PHYSICAL HEALTH

This seems so obvious, but it is surprising to me to meet pastors who seem to function as latter-day Gnostics, ignoring the body, focusing only on the spirit. But of course we exist in a body, and everything we do—whether preaching, praying, or serving—is done in the body. Our ministry is only as good as our body. It is enough that we should care for this one and only earthly body that we have, for our sake, our family's sake, and for the Lord's sake. However, for those pastors who need another reason, I say some of our best ministry opportunities and sermon illustrations may come from times spent running road races, working out at a local gym, or backpacking in the mountains.

PERSONAL FINANCIAL HEALTH

Along with the false, gnostic theology of the physical body, I feel there is also a false, and widespread, theology of money among pastors that borders on asceticism. In his book "Thou Shall Prosper," Rabbi Lappin talks about the discomfort with money that rabbis traditionally had. He even cites his own experience of choosing to be bi-vocational so that he could offer his ministry free to his congregation. He later realized this was a false theology and addresses the unease that many clergy have with money. The fact that we receive our livelihood from the flock we serve can make us feel awkward about money. As pastors, we are tempted to keep our financial affairs as private as possible, lest our flocks feel we have too much. We often feel uncomfortable preaching about money because our motives may be questioned. Our congregation's giving impacts our livelihood.

I coach pastors to adopt the following common sense practices about their finances.

Pay God First

Tithe your income. I am familiar with the discussion about whether tithing belongs to the Old Testament or is applicable today. I just like the simplicity of it. We can talk all we want about Jesus commending the widow for giving everything, but most Christians never get close to tithing let alone giving all. When you tithe personally, you can ask your people with credibility to follow the biblical mandate as well.

Pay Yourself Second, and Live on the Rest

My Norwegian grandmother taught me this. She was well educated in Norway, but because she came to this country as a young adult, her language skills were never good enough for her to work as anything more than a domestic servant. On her small part-time earnings and her husband's factory worker salary, they helped all five of their children get a higher education, either business school or college. After my grandmother was widowed young, she continued to work as a domestic. She supported her church first; then she "paid herself" second, by disciplined savings. Then, last of all, she paid her bills. She lived frugally and was able to help all her children buy homes and her ten grandchildren go to college. We hear a lot about "paying God," but we do not hear as much about "paying yourself."

Someday pastors may want to own their own homes, send their children to college, retire from full-time ministry. Having paid yourself over the years will help you do it. I know the word *retirement* is not in the bible, and I am glad I am still able to work. However, the day will come when you do not have the strength to pastor effectively and then you should retire. An executive minister for a national denomination recently told me that one-third of the 100 pastors in his jurisdiction are no longer effective and should retire because they holding back their churches. He said they are just marking time, many unable to retire because they were not able to put aside enough money during their working life. This is not a good situation for the pastor or the church.

For my wife and me, the simplest budget to practice is 10-10-80. Give to God the first 10 percent. Then give to yourself by saving the second 10 percent. And manage to live on the 80 percent that is left.

Dallas Willard, the late professor of philosophy at UCLA and Christian author, once said, "It is the responsibility of every Christian to carve out a soul-satisfying life, under the rule of God, so sin won't look so good." This profound truth reminds us of our responsibility to care for ourselves and our families so that we will be able to stay healthy in every way and serve God for as long as He allows.

CONCLUSION

One of the most familiar chapters in the Old Testament is Ecclesiastes 3, "There is a season for everything," made famous by a popular song many years ago. It declares that God has purposely designed life and everything in it to have seasons. There are different seasons in the year, in our lives, and in churches. In this book we have attempted to describe and understand the various seasons in the rebirth of a dying church.

The author of Ecclesiastes, King Solomon, points out the ambivalence in each season of life—"a time to be born and a time to die." There is no perfect season. Childhood is filled with the wonder and adventure of youth, but also the confusion of adolescence. Young adulthood is the season of generativity, but it is also the time of juggling and managing all of life's tasks. Old age is the season of wisdom, but also of declining health. So too every season of a church's life is filled with joys and fraught with problems. There is no ideal season, so we are not to wish away any season but to stay present for what God is going to do.

Solomon also declares that God has made "everything beautiful in its time." The Hebrew word for *beautiful* here means "apt, or just right." It is the sense we have about a beautiful picture or a beautiful face—that there is a "just rightness" about it; every feature is in the right place. Every season of the year has its beauty. In northern New England where I live, we have a very short spring, a pleasant temperate summer, a glorious fall, and a long winter. However, even in winter there is beauty. The sunsets are vivid, the night sky is star-filled, the snow reflecting sunlight is diamond bright. There is always a beauty to be found, but sometimes you have to look hard for it.

My prayer is that more pastors will discern and wholeheartedly accept a call to be patient catalysts. Further, I pray that this little volume will help them understand their church's season in the renewal process and that they will trust God's work in that season, knowing that Jesus has declared for all time, and in all seasons, "I will build my Church."

BIBLIOGRAPHY

Barna Group. *Barna Trends 2017: What's New and What's Next at the Intersection of Faith and Culture.* Grand Rapids, MI: Baker Books, 2016.

Bickers, Dennis. *The Healthy Small Church.* Kansas City, MO: Beacon Hill Press, 2005.

Buchanan, Mark. *The Rest of God.* Nashville, TN: Thomas Nelson, 2006.

—. *Spiritual Rhythm.* Grand Rapids, MI: Zondervan, 2010.

Burns, Bob, Chapman, Tasha D., and Guthrie, Donald D. *Resilient Ministry.* Downers Grove, IL: Intervarsity Press, 2013.

Callahan, Kennon L. *Twelve Keys to an Effective Church.* New York, NY: Harper Collins Publishers, 1983.

Campbell, Regi. *Mentor Like Jesus.* Nashville, TN: B & H Publishing Group, 2009.

Collins, Jim. *Good to Great.* New York, NY: Harper Collins Publishers, 2001.

Davis, John Jefferson. *Worship and the Reality of God.* Downers Grove, IL: Intervarsity Press, 2010.

Edwards, J. Kent. *Deep Preaching: Creating Sermons That Go Beyond the Superficial.* Nashville, TN: B & H Publishing Group, 2009.

Fortune, Marie M. *Healthy Boundaries for Clergy and Spiritual Teachers.* Seattle, WA: Faith Trust Institute, 2008.

Foster, Richard J. *Celebration of Discipline.* San Francisco, CA: Harper and Row Publishers, 1978, 1988.

Friedman, Edwin H. *Generation to Generation.* New York, NY: The Guilford Press, 1985, 2011.

Gladwell, Malcolm. *The Tipping Point.* New York, NY: Little, Brown, 2000, 2013.

Harrell, Jim. *Church Replanter.* Rowley, MA: Overseed Press, 2014.

Kaiser, Walter C., Jr. *Quest for Renewal.* Chicago, IL: Moody Press, 1986.

Kotter, John P. *Leading Change.* Boston, MA: Harvard Business Review Press, 1996, 2012.

Lapin, Daniel. *Thou Shall Prosper.* Hoboken, NJ: John Wiley and Sons, 2002.

MacDonald, Gordon. *Who Stole My Church?* Nashville, TN: Thomas Nelson, 2007.

Malphurs, Aubrey. *Planting Growing Churches for the 21st Century: A Comprehensive Guide for New Churches and Those Desiring Renewal.* Grand Rapids, MI: Baker Books, 2004.

Martin, Kevin E. *The Myth of the 200 Barrier.* Nashville, TN: Abingdon Press, 2005.

Martin, Ralph P. *The Worship of God.* Grand Rapids, MI: Wm. B. Eerdmans Publishing Co., 1982.

—. *Worship in the Early Church.* London: Marshall, Morgan & Scott, 1964, 1985.

Maxwell, John C. *Mentor Like Jesus.* Nashville, TN: B & H Publishing Group, 2009.

McConnell, William. *Renew Your Congregation: Healing the Sick, Raising the Dead.* St. Louis, MO: Chalice Press, 2007.

McKinley, Mike. *Church Planting Is For Wimps.* Wheaton, IL: Crossway, 2001.

Osborn, Larry. Sticky Church. Grand Rapids, MI: Zondervan, 2008.

—. *Sticky Teams.* Grand Rapids, MI: Zondervan, 2010.

Peck, Scott M. *The Road Less Traveled.* New York, NY: Simon and Schuster, 1978.

—. *People of the Lie.* New York, NT: Simon and Schuster, 1983.

Pickowicz, Nate. *Revitalize New England.* Entreating Favor, 2017.

Rainer, Thom S. *Autopsy of a Deceased Church.* Nashville, TN: B & H Publishing Group, 2014.

—. *Who Moved My Pulpit?* Nashville, TN: B & H Publishing Group, 2016.

Scazzero, Peter. *The Emotionally Healthy Church.* Grand Rapids, MI: Zondervan, 2003.

Schaller, Lyle E. *Strategies for Change.* Nashville, TN: Abingdon Press, 1993.

Schwarz, Christian A. *Natural Church Development.* St. Charles, IL: Church Smart Resources, 2000.

Slosser, Bob. *Miracle in Darien.* Plainfield, NJ: Logos International, 1979.

Tripp, Paul David. *Dangerous Calling.* Wheaton, IL: Crossway, 2012.

Warren, Rick. *The Purpose Driven Church.* Grand Rapids, MI: Zondervan, 1995.

Webber, Robert. *Planning Blended Worship: The Creative Mixture of Old and New.* Nashville, TN: Abingdon Press, 1998.